Gifted Children
and Their Problems

By the same author:

The Fugitive Mind:
the early development of an autistic child

and

Children Apart:
problems of early separation from parents

Gifted Children
and Their Problems

by Peter Rowlands

J. M. Dent & Sons Ltd
London

First published 1974
© Peter Rowlands, 1974

Made in Great Britain
at the
Aldine Press · Letchworth · Herts
for
J. M. DENT & SONS LTD
Aldine House · Albemarle Street · London W1X 4QY

This book is set in 12 on 13 pt Joanna 478.

ISBN: 0 460 04168 1

108, 493

Contents

Foreword

by the Director of the National Association for Gifted Children

If there had been as readable and sympathetic a book as this one when many of us started teaching in the thirties the whole pattern of our results might have been markedly different. I, for one, would have realized very much sooner the folly of ignoring gifted children and of leaving them to reap the harvest of their talents without my ever trying seriously to understand their special needs. These very few were the fortunate ones who should naturally get on and use their ability so as to bring honour to school and family.

Many did just this, and a number petered out later. Some failed to burgeon and are going to be hampered all through life by feeling they could have done better. Why this wastage? Because, until not so long ago, there was a relentless apathy to the notion of giftedness, tinged not infrequently with a touch of hostility. Teachers after many years' service were genuinely of the impression that they had never run across any gifted children, so the problem was minimal and none of their concern. But let us not forget that these children can under-achieve so superbly well as to go unnoticed. How many were missed? How many were so frustrated that they redirected their talent into wrong channels?

Now public opinion is more realistic. Headmasters and Headmistresses of large comprehensive schools are determined to care as best they can for both ends of the intellectual spectrum. Young teachers are growing into a state of greater awareness and far more student teachers are joining the NAGC because they are engaged on research about gifted children. The considerable interest taken in this area by Mr John Burrows, formerly Chief HMI Primary Education, has been of great assistance in establishing a link between the Department of Education and Science and the NAGC. The same interest is being shown by the HMI who has now succeeded Mr Burrows in looking after the interests of gifted children at the DES. Also Health Services and allied disciplines are concerned in examining how more can be done towards early recognition of these children whom doctors call 'alert babies'. The pre-school years are important not only for the child himself but for the parents too. They can begin to adjust to earlier and more incessant communication and unusual demands all round. They may have to face up to aggression and tantrums, but here the following overriding consideration must be borne in mind:

Of the estimated 182,000 gifted children now at school (the top 2 per cent) it is only a minority, perhaps not even a quarter, who are likely to suffer from disturbances. The remainder are a joy to home and school and are blessed with such a social sense that they are very seldom spoilt or unpopular. Despite any evidence to the contrary, I have encountered quite a number of these children gifted right across the board. They never spare themselves and my only fear for them is that during adolescence they can get very physically tired.

Peter Rowlands has written a book of particular significance at a time when this island has never been in greater need of husbanding its natural resources and ensuring that ignorance will no longer play any part in squandering its best potential. I hope that *Gifted Children and Their Problems* will be widely read, not only by parents and teachers of gifted children but by all who are interested in the very diversity of education and the future of our country.

HENRY COLLIS

27 John Adam Street, London WC2N 6HX
October 1973

Preface

There are not many children in an average school who can be called 'gifted'. Using the definition explained in this book, there might be two in about a hundred children. Because of 'creaming off', some schools will not have any, while others will have a rich mixture of gifted and near-gifted. But many such children are unnoticed, by either parents or teachers. Any attention they attract may be directed at their disturbed behaviour, or their apparent inability to progress in a conventional academic way.

Out of a child population of 15 million in Great Britain, it follows that there are about 300,000 gifted children under the age of fifteen. Many of them have reached or are heading for frustration and unhappiness, while others may veer towards a more comfortable but bleak mediocrity because they can feel safer and more popular if they are inconspicuous. They are a minority group, but a large one, and many of them are at risk.

These were the main thoughts in my mind when I started this book. I would like it to be of help to parents, teachers, and perhaps others, towards understanding more about gifted children. This means getting to know what kind of children they are, what sort of problems they have and what the reasons might be. It is not an exhaustive treatise: it is more of an introduction. There are others better qualified to go deeper into clinical, psychological and educational detail.

A major problem in writing about children is the choice of pronouns. I refuse to refer to a child as 'it'; and saying 'he (or she)' each time is clumsy. I therefore use 'he' almost throughout, although there are obviously as many gifted girls as boys.

I am very grateful to a large number of teachers, psychologists and local education officials who have helped and encouraged me. Special thanks are due to the parents and children who gave me their time, and whose anonymity I have tried hard to preserve. I also want to thank specifically Margaret Branch, Henry Collis, Jean Croft, Gertrude Keir, D. T. E. Marjoram, Marjorie Rowbottom, H. John Taylor, Phyllis Wallbank, Bill Wilks and Bob Woods for putting themselves out to help me. I also thank Susi Hock for all she has done.

One
What is a gifted child?

Just as some children have always, for one reason or another, been less able than others to tackle problems that need intelligence, so there have always been some who have shown themselves to be very much more able than the rest. These have been called by all sorts of names in the past. But 'gifted children' is the term that has currency now. It has drawbacks, in that it arouses antagonism, but it conveys the right meaning to most people. In one way it is a particularly good name for them. A 'gift' may be used or not used, appreciated or not recognized. This certainly goes for these children. Some are top of their class, confident, popular with their friends as well as their teachers, and emotionally secure at home. If somebody calls them 'gifted', it comes as no surprise. But others are very different—to the point that both parents and teachers are completely incredulous at the suggestion that there could be anything gifted about them at all.

Not everyone is happy at the idea that some children should have a special advantage over others. It seems unfair, not to say undemocratic, that some should start life better equipped for academic success or for making a creative or artistic contribution to our society. They are, obviously, more likely to be 'winners': to win scholarships, to be favoured in the academic rat-race, to make a good impression at colleges, in laboratories and in industry, and to enjoy the rewards that tend to come more easily to anyone who makes this kind of progress—more money, more interesting and more secure employment, and more status in society. Winners tend to be respected. At the very least, other people want them on their side. All this makes them an élite. Anyone who feels strongly about equality of opportunity in society, about eliminating inequality and class consciousness, may be distrustful of the idea that there should be a small group of children who are specially equipped for success. But disliking the principle cannot refute the evidence that it exists.

Moreover, helping these children to develop their full potential does not necessarily make them an élitist group, despising the ordinary creatures who cannot aspire to their situation. It *can*, and it probably often *has*: but this can be avoided.

The evidence points to there being two main types of gifted children. One is very quick to learn and make use of whatever is given or shown to him. He builds on his knowledge very capably, and, while he responds well to new material, he enjoys demonstrating easily and impressively how well he has grasped the ideas, principles, skills and procedures that he has already been taught. He has high 'intelligence', in the sense that he performs extremely well at intelligence tests. On the Binet scale, he will score over 140. The second type will not necessarily show up so brilliantly in IQ terms—although he is likely to do very well. He has gifts that are more creative, more original and more exploratory than the ability to do excellent work within a given frame of reference. He will not be recognized for what he is so easily in the classroom—except where the atmosphere favours the non-conformist being noticed for producing work or pursuing interests that are outside what is expected.

This is not to deny that some children are creatively gifted as well as having easily recognizable high intelligence. But with most gifted children there is a tendency for the balance to be clearly in one direction rather than the other.

Bob

Bob is twelve years old. He is a large boy for his age, and looks slightly podgy. But his back is straight and he is one of the fastest runners in his class. The striking thing about him when you first meet is the way he is confident about talking to adults, dismissing what he is doing in a matter-of-fact way, and expressing an alert but polite curiosity in what you are doing yourself. It seems like a meeting between experts who are only different in terms of age.

Yet once he is with his friends, playing football or simply chasing each other round the garden, Bob seems little different from other boys. He plays as hard as he works, and he runs wild in the same way as the other children in the neighbourhood. Seeing him like that, you appreciate that he is, basically, a twelve-year-old, with all the energy that a twelve-year-old needs to release, and the lapses in behaviour that very few twelve-year-olds avoid, and most seem to need.

Unlike the others, Bob is already an academic to be reckoned with. He started reading at four. When he was obviously well able to recognize words from the television screen and cereal packets, his mother got him the first books in the Ladybird reading series, and taught him some words by a simple 'look-and-say' method. In a sense, it was her undoing: Bob devoured the early books at speed and followed her round the house demanding help with others that were a long way ahead of him. She became a prisoner of his fascination for reading.

He imitated long words and copied writing well before he could understand the principles behind either. Pressure on his parents made them help him with his name, shopping lists and letters to relatives, in that order.

When he went to primary school, his precociousness did not go down well with everybody. One teacher realized he had a reading age of about nine or ten, but still insisted that he should join in with the rest of the class following her lessons in the Initial Teaching Alphabet. Bob's parents asked the headmaster politely if it was desirable that their son should be bored stiff with what seemed totally unnecessary preliminaries to reading and writing. He saw their point and intervened, suggesting that Bob should be allowed to read books that interested him during these lessons, and his teacher undertook to talk to him about his reading for short spells during the week. Fortunately there were two others in the class who were early readers, so that there was a group who would benefit from the change.

The headmaster took a strong interest in the future plans and prospects of all his pupils. In Bob's case he was struck by the fact that Bob seemed able to out-perform all his classmates in whatever activity the class was doing. He did not believe in using a marking system, or awarding places in primary school, although the last-year children were given practice in examinations so that future tests would not alarm them. But the difference between Bob's work and the others' spoke for itself. In arithmetic, he advanced to the more difficult Nuffield 'cards' long before the others. He clearly needed to advance quickly, if he was going to be happy, and so he was allowed to do so. In nature study, he made the more comprehensive collections of leaves, and studied rock formations with all the enthusiasm of a determined geologist. In writing, he often made spelling errors because he was constantly trying out new words and expressions in his 'diary' and his stories. But he usually made errors only *once*.

On the headmaster's recommendation, Bob was taken at nine to see an educational psychologist who worked for the local education authority. He was given two tests, on the results of which he was judged to have an IQ of between 140 and 150 (Raven, and Terman-Merrill, respectively). That is to say, he was among the top half per cent of the population in intelligence terms.

There was a lot of hard thinking for the headmaster and his parents to do. What kind of school would be best for him? To help him to make the most of his time at the primary school, the headmaster made two arrangements. Bob was given some special projects in subjects he liked for him to carry out, and then report back to his class. This meant that the class did not suffer, while Bob did not lose interest through the pace being too slow. There was also a scheme operated at a nearby college for very bright children to be allowed to attend small classes in the science block. Although Bob was a bit under age for this, his headmaster made out a special case for him. It worked out very well. But *after* primary school there would not be much choice, if he was to remain within the state system. Two local schools, a former grammar and a secondary modern, were in the process of becoming a comprehensive unit. In time this might become a strong school; but meanwhile half the grammar school teachers had left and the size of classes was kept in check only by use of supply teachers. If it was a risk to send an average child there, it seemed a complete gamble to entrust a very bright child to it.

The headmaster recognized that long-term, successful state education needs to provide for and benefit children of all kinds and degrees of talent. But he felt his first duty was to Bob, and indeed it was to each of his children as individuals. Knowing that academic standards and discipline had dropped sharply at the new comprehensive, he urged Bob's parents to plan for Bob to go to a public school.

The problem was money rather than lateness of application. Bob's father is an aircraft designer: being in an industry that has known better times and having two other children makes one think twice about taking on a heavy financial burden. Obviously it is equally possible to find unsuitable education in a public school too. All the more exasperating, then, to pay for the privilege.

Many public schools offer scholarships to children clever enough to win them, but these by no means cover the cost of private schooling. In fact it makes them more like tokens of approval. In a few cases, however, a child who reaches this standard may have part or all of the expense involved in keeping him at the school paid by the school, which applies its own form of means test. And this, in fact, is what is happening in Bob's case. The school which is taking Bob is well known for showing particular interest in the needs of children with special abilities. It was also prepared to waive Latin as a requirement given that Bob's work in French, along with his other subjects, showed such promise.

Bob is looking forward to going to his new school. He has some regrets about boarding, and about losing his local friends. But he is very positive about the future, and seems determined to get fun out of life as well as to delve deep into the many aspects of art and science that fascinate him.

Gerald

Gerald presents a very different picture. In his second year at primary school his teacher declared that he was a bad influence on the rest of the class and should probably be removed. To what, exactly, she did not specify. She seemed at the end of her tether.

He has never, apparently, been a very easy child to get on with. At seven, he was particularly puzzling. A typical day might start with his refusing to eat breakfast and claiming to be ill. Dispatched to school despite this, he might start by emerging from the cloakroom with his arms tucked down the sides of his sweater, and inside his trousers belt. 'I can't do anything today, Miss! I've got no arms.'

A chorus of other voices would greet him with a mock groan and comments like 'Don't be a lemon!' and 'Trust Gerald!' (He made his classmates laugh sometimes but more often he contrived to exasperate them.)

The teacher might say 'Who wants to get on with their cowboy and Indian pictures?' This referred to a frieze that was being painted in sections as part of a project on the Wild West. She might offer some alternatives and, while little groups formed in different parts of the room, Gerald wandered vacantly from one thing to another.

'You didn't finish your Indian camp bit, did you, Gerald? It was coming on awfully well . . .'

Coaxed, Gerald approached it.

Some time later, the teacher might be collared by a tearful girl, anxious about the future of the project that she and her friends were so proud of: 'Please, Miss Harding, Gerald's spoiling it all.'

'Oh, Gerald!' Pause. 'What is that?'

Gerald would be half nervous, half delighted about what he'd done. 'Well, you see, Miss, a tornado came up and destroyed everything.'

The black whirlpool he had drawn over all his efforts of the previous afternoon was distinctly tornado-ish, once he had explained it. But Miss Harding and his classmates could only see it as a blot on what would otherwise have proved an impressive wall-full at the parents' open day. 'They do have tornados in America,' he added, as a defence against the scorn surrounding him.

Later, in a little group making careful progress towards reading, he would be conspicuous for yawning heavily, and achieving nothing. He distracted some others who tired quickly of reading, and they laughed at him. He wasn't popular with them, however, or with any of the others for that matter. He was somehow different from them.

In the yard, at break, a fight might develop. Sorting the opponents out, Miss Harding would very likely find Gerald at the bottom of the pile.

While others made neat houses with cuisenaire rods, and wrote down the dimensions of the walls, doors and windows, Gerald obviously had other ideas. 'What kind of house is that, Gerald?'

'It's a prison, Miss.'

Although Gerald explained it was easier to measure dimensions if the cells were all the same size and you were looking down on to the top of the prison, it was clear to Miss Harding from his tone of voice that he meant it as an insult too.

The part of school that he liked best was when there was some form of music. He had been known to slip out of his own classroom when he detected that the two senior classes in the school would be listening to some music on the gramophone in the assembly hall. Here he sat in the corner, trying to be as unobtrusive as possible. His habit was discovered in the end when his teacher became suspicious that he was taking about twenty minutes to 'go to the toilet'.

At home, he was equally difficult. He never seemed to

listen to prohibitions: if he was curious about the controls of the television set or the car, he twiddled them. His father had the feeling that punishing Gerald did very little good. He cried, he said he was sorry, then he repeated the act. It seemed possible that Gerald was not so much naughty as mentally handicapped.

His teacher and his parents discussed him, and the possibility of an ESN school was mooted. But this very serious step could not be made before consulting an educational psychologist at the local child guidance centre. This was arranged, when he was just eight.

When it came through, the report staggered everyone. Gerald had proved well above average on a basic intelligence test (involving understanding and use of words, shapes, numbers and general knowledge); he was 'not suitable' for assessment on reading, because he had a specific reading problem; on a mosaic test, in which his use of materials of different kinds was observed, and his explanation of what he was doing was noted, he revealed a higher intelligence than any child the psychologist had ever tested. The report also mentioned a suspicion that he might be musically gifted, that he was an artistic and original thinker with little respect or time for formal teaching, and that he had abnormal emotional problems.

'Well,' said his teacher, 'all this doesn't make him any easier to teach.'

All the same she took advice and gave him some individual help on reading, which took account of the fact that he tended to see words in the reverse, as opposed to their correct order. And she looked for signs of 'artistic and original thinking' in what he did. His parents asked him whether he would like to learn the piano or the violin, and he said he would prefer a French horn (he wanted to be the wolf in *Peter and the Wolf*). He was allowed to join a recorder class higher up the school, and he attended a music centre run at the town hall on Saturday mornings.

Gerald is now thirteen. He is not much more popular than he used to be, but other children recognize that, although he is poor at team games, he is clever at some things, and not just 'odd'. His schoolwork, at a large comprehensive school, is very moderate. His spelling cannot match the kind of expressions he tries to use. His spoken French is reasonably good, but he finds writing it very difficult. Mathematics he enjoys in fits and starts. He has not done much science, but is regarded as promising.

But it is in music that he shines most. He plays the flute really well, in addition to three different types of recorder. He still hankers after the French horn, and will no doubt try it some time. He was found at the music centre to have a very fine singing voice. His ear is very sensitive, and he can recognize notes and reproduce them precisely and beautifully.

His parents get on with him better. But, although they like music, they do not play it, and they feel they do not have much contact with their son. Nor are they confident they are doing the best thing in keeping him at his present school. They feel he needs a balanced education—but more music too. They are surprised and rather frustrated that he is not doing better at his school work, or at making friends. This would make it difficult for him to transfer to a public school, even if they could afford it. They approached a specialist music school, but he was not up to their standard.

Their worry is that Gerald will emerge from school with, say, three or four 'O' levels, and possibly one at 'A', which will not be enough for him to go to university. At the same time, he will continue to be very good at music, but not sufficiently trained to make any kind of career in it. 'He looks like falling between two schools,' his father says.

*   *   *

Two very different children. They seem so unlike each other when you meet them that it seems perverse to put them into one category. But they are both, in their separate ways, gifted. Seeing them one after the other is a salutary reminder that gifted children vary, just as all children vary, and that each has his own problems, opportunities and personality.

They are good examples of the 'high IQ' gifted child and the 'creative' child, respectively. However, while there is also evidence of creativity in Bob, there is not so much evidence of academic ability in Gerald—probably mainly because of his reading disability.

Some children of average intelligence (or less) are 'creative' in certain ways. It is consistent originality, fluency of ideas and flexibility of thought combined with high intelligence that are exceptional.

Rather different from the two types discussed so far are those children who are exceptionally talented in one specific direction. This may be in music, ballet or in some form of art or sport. Examples of these will be considered later. They can be very intelligent in a general sense: but they are invariably highly skilled.

Bob and Gerald also exemplify achievement and under-achievement. It is by no means always the case that the high IQ gifted child does better at school (this depends on the school, the teacher, the family and other interests), but because academic work usually involves tests that demand persevering application to work within a given format, the high IQ child will usually be favoured by them.

It is sometimes useful to think of creative children being more inclined to divergence than convergence as thinkers. Bob is rather more convergent, Gerald definitely more divergent, than the other way about. A convergent thinker applies his brain to a situation or a task within a particular setting; the divergent thinker may well query the setting first. Nobody (gifted children included) is entirely the one or the other. But most people have a tendency one way or the other, and research suggests that most people are convergent.

Bob is convergent in applying himself happily to work that is a continuation of what he has started on. He will work logically through a book. He rehearses his knowledge happily, as well, which helps him to pass tests. In short, he accepts the system he is given, and merely asks polite questions when he feels he has met something inconsistent.

Gerald is divergent because he wants to turn the system upside-down every so often. A mural of cowboys and Indians can hold his attention for a while, but then he feels a 'What if . . .?' compulsion to explore the effect of a tornado on the camp. Again, why should he build a house with his rods when everyone else is doing the same? The principle is too easy. But it might be fun (as well as satisfying an urge for revenge) to see if it applies to a prison too.

It is easy to see how useful a brain like Bob's can be for society. In a college, in government, in industry, or wherever —it is going to be capable of assimilating and weighing information, and judging the effects of decisions in the light of this, to a greater extent than other brains (that is, if it develops its potential).

In Gerald's case the pay-off is less easy to define. But somebody has got to jolt Bob's complacency sometim success comes too easily to him. Somebody has got to be abrasive and present an alternative view, if society is not going to fossilize. Somebody has got to extend artistic functions—traditionally this happens in ways that first alarm or shock, and later delight, people. Somebody too has got to have a sceptical turn of mind, and say: 'What if they're *all* wrong? What if *we* go round the *sun*?' That is how progress is made, and Gerald's contribution is needed too.

A lot of suspicion surrounds IQ tests and other assessments made by psychologists. People often ask questions like these: how can they measure every part of intelligence? If somebody does well at an IQ test, what guarantee is there that he is practical, has leadership qualities, or has the determination to put his ideas or beliefs into practice? These points are fair. Psychologists have been trying for many years to improve their tests, and to make them more comprehensive and sensitive. Tests of creativity are, in fact, fairly recent evidence that they are not complacent. But the nature of most tests makes it hard for them to reflect anything more subtle than very obvious aspects of technical flair, or personality. A great deal of what can be very important in life is missed. But this does nothing to refute that IQ itself must mean something. Where a gifted child is concerned, a very high IQ score is a statement that in certain circumstances he is extremely likely to be able to bring a higher level of intelligence to bear on problems than other children. This means he has very high *potential* rather than *active* talent. It is up to others to help him to make his talent active.

In other questions about IQ, parents query whether the results of one IQ test are repeated in another. Is it not possible for a child to have an off day? Will he not do better on one test than another? Can you ever, then, rely on these tests for identifying a gifted child? Assessing giftedness and using these tests is a skilled operation. It is best done on an individual basis, so that the psychologist can note the nervousness, the interest level, and any other factors that could be interfering with a typical result. He will reserve judgment if something is clearly wrong. Moreover, he will almost certainly use more than one test if there is a serious doubt in his mind. It is true that some tests are better for the 'creative' type than the 'high IQ' type. But the degree of correlation between tests where the results for gifted children are concerned is very high. Repeating the same test on a gifted child— or trying a second one on him—is very likely to give much the same picture. Where a gifted child is considerably disturbed or has a particular problem, like Gerald's over reading, a test's reliability may be less certain, but if an individual assessment is being made, a skilled interviewer will not let this confuse the issue.

Assessment of giftedness can be very accurate at a very early age. Up to the age of three, non-talkers can be puzzling. But some research has been accurate, long-term, with 80 per cent of infants. (Testing at an early age is obviously by observation.)

When gifted children are identified, as many boys as girls will be found to qualify. Unlike some people's conception of 'the Owl of the Remove', the gifted child is very likely to have some kind of athletic as well as academic skill. There is some evidence that the number of children with giftedness varies from one culture to another. This may be a different response to parents', teachers' and other children's expectations, quite as much as a difference in basic ability. But this question is under-researched. (There are obvious political reasons why the results of this kind of investigation may be unwelcome in some quarters, *whatever* they show about races.)

Some people who work closely with children of all kinds have noted that gifted children are often calmer, emotionally more stable, and have better social poise than others. Yet other gifted children—by no means always the 'creative' kind—are distinctly disturbed in their emotional development. They can be physically aged seven, mentally (i.e. by test) aged eleven and emotionally aged four. This paradox will be discussed further.

Should we care about identifying gifted children? If they are so good, won't they make headway on their own account? The evidence is that many do *not*. Like Gerald, they are misunderstood, unpopular and sometimes even written off as fools. Education is supposed to mean, nowadays, helping children to realize their potential and lead a fuller life, in social terms and in terms of activities. A child with a special brain needs special help. We do not have so many gifted children that we can afford to squander their talents by making it difficult for them to emerge. In Russia, socialist principles are not regarded as inconsistent with identifying the gifted and discovering appropriate education for them. A great deal of the Russians' technological progress since the war has been ascribed to their success at this. The United States has responded too—shocked by a finding that suggested that over 40 per cent of the gifted children in that country did not go on to college education.

But there is also a humanitarian argument for helping gifted children, which should be more cogent. In a sense, they are handicapped, just as ESN children are. They are handicapped by their ability if they are bound by a school routine that is entirely concentrated on the needs of the average; by low key, repetitive activity that their friends (or even their parents, sometimes) indulge in and value;

systems which block them from exploring new interests, and extensions of their interests, that they can sense, but need help and encouragement to come to grips with. We help mentally handicapped children, because we agree it is only fair to do so. But we are only starting to help those who are handicapped by gift.

Two
What makes a child gifted?

A gifted child is probably gifted from birth. This is the conclusion to be drawn from the fact that predictions made from careful observation of exceptional infants' behaviour tend to be fulfilled over time. For some reason or other, one particular child is born with better mental equipment than most others. Why?

It is very difficult not to believe that genetics play a very big part in this. In 1925 Terman, who made some of the earliest scientific investigations of giftedness, or 'genius', found that a very large proportion of gifted children were born to families in the professional classes. Later work, up to the present day, has done little to disprove the obvious point that professional people were more likely to produce a child with intelligence characteristics that are more associated with that class. But in the past many children in lower-class families had little chance of any gifts they might have had being noticed. With better and fairer means of identification available, it now seems that most gifted children come from the families of semi-professional people. Since this group is far larger than the professional, its contribution to the pool of gifted children is greater. But conversely, relatively few gifted children are found to come from the even larger group of non-white-collar workers. This is by no means conclusive evidence (since it could be a measure of differences in treating young children, as well as of genetic differences), but it offers some support to the genetic argument.

A professional couple may have a mentally handicapped child, be he mongol, or feeble-minded, or autistic. This could happen to them, just as it does to other couples. Might this be an argument against genetic determination of giftedness?

One theory suggests that families have a long-term tendency to 'even out' in intelligence. This may happen over several generations and depends on factors such as the kind of new blood that is introduced. If intelligence does 'even out' this would account for the presence within the same professional family of one child who was much more intelligent than the average, and one who was distinctly less so. But this whole area is very speculative. Again, genetics can be politically a hot subject.

One educational psychologist with many years of experience of identifying and helping gifted children maintains that responsibility for a child being gifted is roughly 80 per cent vested in heredity, and only about 20 per cent in upbringing. When asked why, he stopped short of committing 100 per cent to heredity, but explained his view further: the genes do in fact exclusively determine giftedness but, in a few cases, the upbringing factors are bad enough to nip it in the bud or make it unrecognizable. That is to say, the 20 per cent is not a case of an ungifted child being 'promoted' to the gifted category by astute upbringing. The 20 per cent is purely a negative concept. This psychologist is unwilling for his opinion to go on record, for two reasons. Firstly, it is not the kind of theory that is likely to be proved or disproved. Secondly, because it is unfashionable in educational circles to imply openly that educational opportunities are not equal for all children, or that there is any substance in the idea that one social class is more intelligent than another.

A hereditary factor need not necessarily be the same thing as a genetic likelihood for the upper middle class to produce gifted children. For example, mixing blood in particular ways (e.g. *between* social classes, or racial groups) may logically improve a family's chances of increasing its proportion of highly intelligent members within a given generation.

Some other evidence implies indirectly but clearly that high intelligence may be transmitted by parents. Admittedly one or two assumptions are needed—particularly that high intelligence is more often found among those who are in the professions or have reached a higher level of education. A study of cases where children with a poor record at school have been referred to clinics for guidance and are subsequently found to have a 'gifted' IQ should in theory supply relevant evidence. After all, they were a mystery to those controlling their environment and often they were accepted as 'backward'. Therefore the possibility that intellectual environment (at home or at school) was the major factor in their giftedness must seem at least diminished if not eliminated. The family characteristics ought, then, to have meaning in themselves.

M. L. Kellmer Pringle made a close study of over a hundred gifted children among the many who had been referred to her clinic. Her study had nothing to do with the argument discussed here, but a separate look at her data is suggestive. Of all the children she saw, those who proved to be gifted more often than is likely by chance came from families where one parent or both were in a profession, had been to a grammar school, or had received further education. Normally it can be argued that this kind of parent is more concerned with his children's education anyway—which increases the chance of their being referred. This seems to me much less likely in these cases. (However, Dr Kellmer Pringle herself points out that this is not a watertight argument: theoretically, working-class parents may have been more likely to refuse permission for their child to attend the clinic, or to have ignored appointments.)

It is much more common for people to agree that specific talents or gifts can be passed on from parents to children, than for them to agree that overall intelligence is simply transmitted. There are many cases of musical families (from the Bachs onwards) where one generation after another takes up an instrument, or sings, or makes some other kind of study of music. Those who have a skill at drawing, or other forms of art, often seem to be related to others with a similar skill. This is accepted, as a plausible hereditary trait, almost like having red hair, or good eyesight. (Environment may of course contribute to the continuation of artistic or musical activity in a family, but that is not the point.) Certain types of illness, including mental illness, run through families, although not entirely predictably. It seems logical that other kinds of mental make-up may be passed on, which are more difficult to isolate and assess. These might include a tendency towards greater general intelligence. However, it is less satisfactory for many people to admit that high intelligence may run in families, like perfect musical pitch or a mechanical skill. This is because it is socially divisive to suggest that certain families may be better fitted to produce leaders in industry, learning or politics. Such divisions are suspect, because they may be used as reasons for furthering inequalities between children. What research there is, all the same, suggests that parents differ both in what they pass on genetically to their children as well as in what they actually *do* with them, and how they help them.

In a sense, this nature versus nurture problem is not really worth much thought, if one's concern is to be practical. Nobody can change what the genes have produced, and nobody but an extremist can think in terms of 'eugenics', or planning families in order to procreate only the most intelligent. What is possible is to try to understand one's own children, and help them to get the best that they can out of their talents, and out of their life.

Parents who have not had a child before are not in an ideal position to recognize a young child's intellectual potential. They will usually be so much in love with him that pride in his achievements prevents their making any kind of critical assessment, even in comparison with other children of similar ages. Lots of mothers who take their child to a kindergarten for the first time are surprised at what they see: over there is a little girl who seems younger but runs *faster* than her Johnny, and some little voice is using words that sound every bit as precocious as those which Johnny uses. Such a mother is beginning to see her child (or children) in a broader context. But her reaction is often to suppose that 'they must be a very bright lot at this kindergarten', rather than to draw the conclusion that Johnny may be average.

Then there are parents who are disappointed in their children. A child may be the wrong sex, or look less lovable than had been expected; he may be slower than imagined, or more trouble. Rather commonly, arguments about such a child may be part of a long-term matrimonial wrangle which makes the child an object of resentment, at least to one parent if not to both. In such a family, even when a child does or says things that imply that he may be exceptional, little notice is taken of them. He is still criticized for not being what they would like him to be.

Parents with several children at least have the opportunity to compare their children's progress from the start. But because they themselves have probably improved—at handling temper tantrums, helping a child to walk and talk, and at giving him things to do which stimulate him and prevent boredom—they may also get a false idea of a younger child being 'much quicker than Johnny ever was'. It is a short step from here to assume that this younger child must be gifted.

Yet the point was made in the last chapter that giftedness can be spotted very early on. If not by the parents—by whom? The answer, unfortunately, is by educational psychologists. A teacher can sometimes have a very clear impression of a child's ability, but is more likely to spot ability that is readily reflected in good school work, such as Bob's in chapter 1. There are many cases where Gerald's kind of gift is not suspected by teachers because it does not fit their pattern. Some preliminary findings from a large-scale experiment organized by Professor Tempest at Southport suggest that only half of the gifted children identified conclusively as such by the experiment were noted as gifted by their teacher. Teachers therefore vary in their reliability. Their evidence—what they have to say about a child's work in school—is often invaluable to an educational psychologist because it adds a dimension to what he is building up. But teachers are more likely to be emotionally involved than the psychologist, who is asked to make a brief but thorough acquaintance of a child, test him and make an assessment. He has at his disposal a range of tests which have themselves been tested for reliability, for the ways in which they agree and disagree with each other and for their predictive value over time. He has also learnt to be distrustful of situations where children are tested in groups, since it is established that some children are simply not motivated to do their best in group tests. So he will want to make an individual test before he commits himself to a judgment, and he will take into account any factors which he thinks may be affecting the score, such as whether or not the child can read yet.

But, even before a child is 'testable' in this sense, a lot can be determined by skilled observation.

A very young child's intelligence cannot be judged purely and simply in terms of his speech, or his answers to questions. Even very bright children vary considerably in the age at which they suddenly start displaying intelligent vocal efforts. And the younger the child, the greater the chance of misunderstandings or emotional problems getting in the way of conducting an accurate test along formal lines.

Ruth Griffiths followed others in recognizing that valuable clues to a child's likely ability could be gained by watching him carefully: noting how he moved, how he approached new toys and how he responded to other people. But she systematized her observation into a scheme which allowed a point score to be built up for children even one or two months old. The scheme involved awarding points according to performance of particular acts, relative to the child's age. The acts were divided into five broad areas:

LOCOMOTION   *examples*: *a* lifting the head
                                      (expected in 2nd month)
                                   b jumping
                                      (20th month)
PERSONAL/SOCIAL *examples*: *a* recognizing   mother   by
                                      sight
                                      (2nd month)
                                   b bladder control by day
                                      (20th month)
HEARING/SPEECH *examples*: *a* monosyllabic
                                      (2nd month)
                                   b vocabulary of 30 words
                                      that he can use
                                      (20th month)

EYE AND HAND	examples:	a	follows a ring moved up and down
			(2nd month)
		b	pours water from one cup to another
			(20th month)
PERFORMANCE	examples:	a	moving his arms vigorously
			(2nd month)
		b	turning a screw
			(24th month)

Much of this may seem physical rather than mental. But accomplishment of most physical tasks by young children involves understanding of what is to be done and, more gradually, how best to do it. Children who are forward in these attainments as infants are very often showing that they have the potential for understanding things, and acting on them, more quickly than others. Later this gets translated into more obvious marks of intelligence.

In 1969 Donald Kincaid reported on a study of 'highly gifted' children in the Los Angeles area, USA. He analysed information on over 500 children between six and twelve who were found by test to have an IQ of 150 or more. These in fact formed a more exclusive group than the 'gifted' children discussed in this book: they are fewer than 1 in 1,000. Kincaid found that, among these children, the average age for starting to walk was 11.7 months (girls) and 11.8 months (boys). Most children are at least 12 months old before they can walk at all when taken by the hand, and independent walking is more normal from 14 months onwards. This supports the proposition that the very intelligent child is likely to be advanced in these physical activities. As might be expected, Kincaid's group were also advanced in learning to talk and to read.

It must be remembered, however, that this is a question of *averages*. Not every gifted child will be quick to master new physical problems; some may inherit personality or physical characteristics (as well as intelligence) which pull the other way. Also, any child will reach physical skills more quickly with appropriate help.

There is a big difference between making meticulous notes about movements, responses to parents and other children and so forth as a detached observer, and getting a feeling for a child's character. Understanding in what *ways* a child might be gifted depends on looking for his personality development too.

Parents have very uncertain memories, but they can often supply important clues about the kind of child they have by noting and talking about what his mood is *generally* like, what his dislikes and preferences *usually* are, and what is his customary way of dealing with a new problem. This kind of information is taken into account by an educational psychologist, not because everything the parent says is right, but because the descriptions used by the parent tell him whether there is likely to be something unusual in the child's performance or character; whether the child is different on the day of interview; how variable in temperament he is (which will obviously affect performance on tests); and what kind of feelings predominate between parent and child. It is rather like a doctor listening to a patient who has come in for a consultation about a pain in his chest: he pays attention not so much to details of self-diagnosis as to the tone of voice, what the words suggest about the patient's normal health, and how far they coincide with other patients' expressions when talking about what turned out to be indigestion, cancer, hypochondria, etc.

Parent and patient both have important information to give
—but it requires skilled interpretation.

Jim

Here is one mother's account of her gifted son as a young
infant. She is intelligent, and likely to be right in many of
her impressions. Although she has simplified her picture of
Jim in certain respects, references to the diary she kept of his
progress and cross-checking with friends and other members
of the family show that there is unlikely to have been much
distortion.

Jim's IQ has been tested twice: once in a group test at his
primary school, and once individually by an educational
psychologist. He was well into the 'gifted' category both
times. He has just started at a public school, after winning a
scholarship to go there. His ability is general, across all
subjects, although he prefers maths. His mother has these
recollections of him as a young child:

> Jim was very curious as a child. Unlike Mary [his sister],
> who always accepted everything as though it was the
> natural order of things, Jim peered at you intently, as if
> sizing up what you were doing, and whether you were
> doing it right. I can see him now, peering round at me
> from his high chair, watching me spoon his baby food out
> of the can, and test its warmth against my wrist. You felt
> he would notice if you did something wrong.
>
> He wasn't terribly quick at standing up, and walking.
> But he could use his hands very quickly. He got them into
> everything. In his high chair, he always wanted to probe
> and pinch at his food, as well as eat it—almost like a
> weights and measures inspector! He was good at making

towers of bricks. I remember, when he could only sit up, he would make a tower as high as he could reach, and then shuffle around it, wondering how he could get another brick on top. Jigsaws he was good at too. He was always interested in tackling his elder sister's jigsaws although they were supposed to be too old for him . . . actually, he was *always* interested in trying older children's toys.

He talked pretty quickly, I suppose. He could give you a lot of sensible conversation at eighteen months. He used to get accepted into the games Mary played with the children across the way where they had to imagine things happening to them (like Mothers and Fathers, and a story about a witch they used to try to escape from every week). The other smallies weren't allowed in. Jim got very disappointed when the other children were not there one day, and he was told they were at school.

I'm probably making you feel he was always at the centre of things, talking a lot and making friends. This wasn't so. He was often very quiet, particularly if he'd found something to get his teeth into. If he was drawing something, or trying to make a large animal out of Lego, he used to work at it very carefully, for a long time. In fact he used to get carried away by what he was doing much more than his sister.

It was a surprise to find that he'd learnt to read some words almost entirely by himself. I say 'almost', because Mary and perhaps Mary's friends helped him. When they watched television together, he picked some words up from the screen. He learnt that D-R W-H-O is 'Dr Who', and that F-L-A-K-E is the chocolate bar, and so on. I noticed this when he pointed to a headline in the *Radio Times* as I was looking through it and he said, 'That says Dr Who'. He was about three and a half. After that I helped with some Dick Bruna books, and he could soon read confidently by himself.

He wasn't a goody-goody child, I'm glad to say. He was naughty, he got bored and cried; he quarrelled with his sister; he could tease other children and punched them up once or twice; and he went through a phase of being rude to any visitors. But he was never really bad for long.

There are several points about this description of Jim that are worth noting because they reflect some basic features of young gifted children.

'Jim was very curious . . .' Lots of young babies are curious about this and that. Parents should not imagine that curiosity means their child must be gifted. But exceptional curiosity can be an indicator when it goes with a persistence in finding out that often brings him into conflict with parents, who are anxious about his getting into danger. This is proof that the baby is an individual who is determined to be an individual. He is insisting from the earliest moment on developing personal experience.

'. . . peered at you intently, as if sizing you up . . .' A young gifted child often *looks* in a way that suggests he wants more than conventional cuddling and baby language. Of course he needs these things just as much as every baby, but he starts to thrive on more mature contact with his parents much earlier on. Some parents, who do not understand their gifted child and how quickly he can become dissatisfied with what is repetitive or has lost interest for him, resent his pert look as a kind of challenge. They feel vaguely threatened by a young child who does not, they feel, behave as a young child *should*. In fact an intelligent look deserves an intelligent word. It is as much a part of loving one's child as cuddling him.

'You felt he would notice if you did something wrong.'

Implicit in this comment is a feeling that Jim noted logical sequences, and expected them to go according to the plan he perceived in them. Gifted children often seem to show an early ability to see what follows what, as well as what goes with what. Sometimes they are classified as having a 'very logical' or 'methodical' mind.

'He wasn't terribly quick at standing up, or walking.' Though they vary in this, many gifted children *do* seem to be quick, agile and well co-ordinated.

'He could use his hands very quickly.' What his mother is saying is that he did things *accurately* with his hands. This means rapid development of eye and hand co-ordination. Gifted children *do* seem to have this very often. It comes out in their early constructional games with bricks and Lego, in playing with balls and friction toys, in their first attempts at representational drawing and in their first efforts towards independence in dressing and undressing.

'He got . . . into everything.' Insatiable curiosity is typical of the gifted child. Not *all the time*, of course. But once something strikes them as interesting, they have to follow it through—either physically or by asking questions.

'Although they were supposed to be too old for him.' Gifted children are often very difficult at birthdays or Christmas time, especially when small, because they don't seem to appreciate their own presents as much as somebody else's. Later, they know how to ask for what interests them. If they are happy playing with what is 'supposed to be' for an older age group, it is obviously wise to let them explore it—within the bounds of safety.

'He talked pretty quickly . . .' This, again, is a sign of a gifted child. The time of most rapid progress (by comparison with others) seems to be at two years, when they are discovering the magic of asking questions and getting answers. Their repertoire then expands very fast.

'. . . sensible conversation'. The use of the word 'sensible' implies that his mother is still rather surprised at the unchildishness of the questions and replies her son makes. Not brilliant conversation, with lots of long words and difficult concepts—just 'sensible', adult-to-adult conversation.

'He used to be accepted . . .' Older children will accept younger children into their games at certain times, for certain reasons. Gifted children fit in more often because they contribute to what is being played, being more articulate and more mature in their reactions. When they play with children their own age, they often have to lead or 'boss' the others, to make the game as interesting as they want it: this can easily lead to friction and resentment.

'. . . carried away by what he was doing'. Gifted children often exhibit intense concentration for longer periods than others seem capable of devoting or willing to devote to a subject. This starts very early on and parents who do not realize it sometimes say a gifted child is 'dreaming', because he doesn't seem to respond to their questions. What is happening is that he is concentrating, and he filters distractions and interruptions out of his consciousness.

'. . . he'd learnt to read some words entirely by himself.' Lots of children do this either before or after they are being taught to read by parents or teacher. Particularly if he is playing with older children, it is often frustrating for a gifted child to be able to read a little but not enough to satisfy his curiosity or to keep up with the others. He needs help then —but not pushing.

'. . . some Dick Bruna books'. Later, when Jim came across standard early readers at his nursery school, he refused to read them, and his teacher did not believe for a while that he could read. Jim's mother had chosen books that had a few long, curious words, as well as simple ones. At three and a half, it might not have mattered, but gifted children sometimes 'fail' to read when the material seems dull or repetitive to them.

'He was naughty.' This comes as a kind of relief. A gifted child can be naughty in all kinds of ways. (This depends on what a parent calls 'naughty'.) Tantrums seem to be as violent and as frequent among the gifted as among others. Negativism may be more peculiar to gifted children: a desire for independence, for concentration on one's own activities and interests. It consists simply of saying 'No' and 'Shan't' rather a lot. Other forms of naughtiness are standardized: hitting brothers and sisters from jealousy, tasting or touching what is forbidden, trying out rudeness to see what effect it has—all these are perfectly normal.

'. . . never really bad for long'. This may be more like a gifted child, although again it is not an exclusive indication. Gifted children seem to be better able, on the whole, to come to terms with whatever is opposing them and adapt their behaviour so that they are not bad-tempered or difficult company for long. Sharper understanding of people and of what reactions follow what behaviour probably contribute most to this.

But not all gifted children present such an impressive picture when very young. Some are distinctly less obvious in their intelligence, distinctly more difficult socially, and present their own brand of problems. This chapter has largely concerned the main stream of gifted children. Later chapters will discuss why some are found in other, more turbulent, streams.

Three
Early developers

The evidence, such as it is, on heredity and on development suggests that a gifted child starts with his built-in advantage which may, or may not, be allowed to develop. Once it starts developing and is appreciated by his family and teachers there is almost certainly progress. This will be faster at certain times than at others, but the movement is almost always definitely forward. There are, however, some cases of unusual early development which deserve consideration before going further.

These problem cases—called such because they do not seem to fit in with a tight, neat theory of giftedness—fall into four categories:

a Some children make spectacular early development, to the extent that, whether they have been formally tested or not, it makes sense to call them gifted. Thereafter (for example from the age of six or seven onwards) they gradually or suddenly seem to lose the head start that they had. Eventually their work, their interests and their ambitions become fixed at or near the average for children of that age.

b Another group demonstrates very early on that they are remarkably gifted in one particular way. Perhaps they play the recorder effortlessly and beautifully. Perhaps they are mathematical 'wizards' with amazing powers of lightning calculation. Yet in other aspects they have average, or below average ability.

c A child may seem to be intelligent, but not gifted, in his early years. Or he may perform well up to the gifted level in tests, but not in general work either at school or on his own. Suddenly he develops one or more talents—academic or otherwise—to a degree that suggests he may be gifted.

d The final category that presents a problem is that of children who are undeniably gifted over a fairly wide or very wide range of pursuits, and yet have one or two 'blind spots'. These may be mathematics, languages, handicrafts—anything, even reading.

Each of these groups raises uncertainties about the notion of 'giftedness' as outlined in the first two chapters. They will now be considered in turn.

a Stars that lose their shine
If a child is gifted from birth, how *can* he stop being so? In cases where a child is ill treated or resented by parents and teachers, there are obvious reasons why this should happen. But that is not the kind of problem at issue here. An ill-treated child's giftedness, if it exists, is unlikely to be noticed unless a local authority investigates and asks for an assessment. Thereafter, provided he can be satisfactorily settled, he will probably improve. What we are talking about here are children who are spotted, one way or another, for being special and endowed at an early stage and, *despite* encouragement, do not achieve as much as was expected of them and decline in their intelligence test rating too.

There are a lot of factors which can encourage a gifted child to under-achieve. They deserve a section to themselves, but it is worth noting here that parents and teachers may be under-stimulating him or over-pressurizing him; he may be in a class where popularity is instantly withdrawn from any boy or girl who 'swots' or does well; or the kind of activity at which a child naturally excels may not be approved by parents or friends for children of that sex—e.g. athletics or metalwork for girls, art or cookery for boys. These are all logical (and unfortunately frequent) reasons why a gifted child might become less conspicuous over time.

It seems logical that children should under-achieve unless something positive is done to encourage them to feel that they *want* to do things more thoroughly, and that there *are* interesting things which are worth knowing more about. But does it follow that children in this situation can actually lose in intelligence, and have less potential than they once had?

This is a theoretical rather than a practical point. But gifted children are often suspected of being likely to 'fizzle out': sometimes, no doubt, by people who resent them or are unwilling to accept that some have superior intelligence that lasts. Where people point to examples of unfulfilled promise, are they looking at intelligence which has 'fizzled out', or intelligence which has been frustrated from showing itself and so is essentially still there?

Where a child has developed a consistent pattern of under-achievement in which he assumes, right at the beginning of any challenge, that he will fail or just scrape through, then even the more sensitive IQ test may get the same low response from him as all his school tests. Effectively, then, his IQ score may be lower by test; therefore the 'gifted' label no longer applies to him. In an individual test, however, as opposed to a group test, a psychologist can observe whether and how far the achieved score seems to be a reflection of ability, motivation or emotional mix-ups. Many cases of apparent loss of giftedness have been instances where factors like these last two seem to be telling against performance.

Certain kinds of giftedness do seem liable to be inhibited by what society, or a school, expects. This kind of loss may be permanent, particularly if the child concerned accepts and repeats his society's expectations. Some years ago an interesting research project was conducted among children of similar ages in families of similar economic status in the following areas: Germany, Australia, the USA, India and Western Samoa. It measured and contrasted creativity, mainly in terms of originality as determined by standardized tests. This is only one aspect of giftedness, but there was one clear-cut result. Whereas children in the USA and Germany demonstrated a high overall level of creativity both in their first year of school and right the way through to their sixth year, in Australia the findings were markedly different. There children started with moderate creativity, on average, which became low when they reached the sixth-year check. Commentators have suggested that this might be a result of Australian school methods being less flexible and less geared to originality, and of pressures even on young children to be conformist rather than innovative. Whatever the reasons, there is a clear indication that creativity can wane given adverse conditions.

But can creativity wane among the gifted? The children in the cross-cultural study above were taken from all levels; theoretically, the average results could have buried and disguised a continuing high level of creativity among a few.

A paper in 1970 by Jon Jacobs reported that out of nineteen children tested before they first went to school, and found to be gifted, only seven managed to maintain their IQ score at a sufficient level to remain in this category once they had been to school for a year. Sounds like a bad school! But these children were at different schools. Moreover, this was in the USA, where a great deal of prominence has been given to the need to spot and encourage gifted children.

It is not easy to know whether this research is pointing more closely at the possibility that early testing of IQ is fallible or that the giftedness of young children can go into an eclipse during a period at a school that is wrong for them. Possibly both points are fair. But the eclipse, if it happens, may not be long-lasting or permanent. An interesting sideline is that none of the nineteen gifted children was recognized by his teacher as being gifted. This is less surprising if one allows for the fact that this was in kindergarten. It suggested to Jacobs that most of the gifted children who have been studied are the kind who are liable to be recognized by teachers, and these may represent an entirely different personality or aptitude group from any talented children entering school for the first time. The suspicion of undiscovered sources of brain power going to waste constantly exercises the minds of workers in this area.

b The 'One-Gun Pete' children

When a child is brought to the notice of a startled public for playing a Beethoven concerto at ten, or for knowing the names of each first team player in every division of the Football Association, or for any similar accomplishment, two thoughts immediately come to mind. The first is that it certainly seems remarkably clever. The second is to ask oneself doubtfully: Is he clever at anything else?

Being clever is not the same as being intelligent. Intelligence adapts to circumstances, and can be applied in many different ways. Cleverness may or may not be limited in the way it can express itself.

Obviously it would be wrong to assume that because a child is precociously clever at some manipulative skill (say, taking small machines to pieces and fitting them together again), this kind of cleverness is the limit of his attainments. Children have been put into arbitrary categories like this, probably since time began. It does them little good to be told 'you are a born mechanical engineer' if the implication is that his brightness lies in twiddling knobs and levers rather than in understanding the theories, physical and mathematical, behind the machines he can cope with. Limiting a child unfairly is wrong. But so is the assumption that he is necessarily displaying an example of high intelligence.

Whether the child is in fact intelligent or not, it is pointless to denigrate a special skill. He has it, it gives him pleasure and it gives other people pleasure too.

Sometimes there are cases when a child is altogether backward in most respects but has a peculiar 'island' of surprising cleverness. This may be a musical skill, or an ability to express emotions in paint on canvas in a vivid and compelling way. For a child who is mentally handicapped, it is particularly wonderful to have a special area in which he can excel and command admiration.

It has been supposed at times that the existence of *idiots savants*, or people who combine expertise in one or a few areas with very low intelligence in all others, suggests that high intelligence and some conditions of mental handicap are closely related. This is entirely speculative, but it is an interesting theory. There is some evidence in both that hereditary factors are involved. The idea that a mental handicap occurs when a particularly subtle brain in its last stages of development in the uterus is subject to stress is not original. It has been put forward as an explanation for autism: some of the supporting evidence being that autistic children sometimes have 'islands' of intelligence despite their very considerable handicap.

This should not let one suppose, however, that gifted children are more likely than others to become mentally ill or emotionally disturbed. Educationists who have observed many of them are inclined to agree that they tend to be emotionally more stable than other children and to be very realistic in their outlook. Some gifted children *are* unstable for particular reasons, which will be discussed later.

c Late Developers
There is not much evidence of 'late development' in the sense of children achieving much better IQ scores (that is, high enough to get them into the 'gifted' category) after being unexceptional at an early age. At the same time, there are cases of children performing markedly better at one kind of test than at another. A good example is where a late reader at the age of six or seven is put through a test that is over-reliant on the use of words. Later on, when interest in reading and using words has caught up, this same child may 'show' a marked improvement in IQ. This can of course happen with a gifted child just as much as with others, and setting him a test that is less concerned with words would give the same kind of result—assuming that he really is gifted. For both, the apparent change of IQ is obviously artificial.

Even when it is suspected that a child may be gifted, or near-gifted, in his overall intelligence it may take a longer time for him to shine at something specific than most people would expect. This is not the same thing as saying that there is one particular talent that he must find if he is to stand out from the rest. What is more likely is that he has suddenly been fired with enthusiasm to deploy his talents in a particular direction.

Gifted children need stimulation to give of their best. Sometimes this happens with relatively little effort on anyone's part. But sometimes they seem to be very choosy about where to bestow their interest and effort (or rather they get rapidly bored by material used successfully with the rest of a class because it seems banal or repetitive to them). They sometimes seem to scorn simple readers because they are considerably ahead of the vocabulary and the context by the time they reach them. You would not take kindly to reading a book about people who you felt were uniformly rather stupid and uninspired.

Absence of appropriate stimulation, then (which may include absence of a teacher who commands interest and respect), may account for many of those who seem to be 'late developers'.

The idea that some of these might be turning into gifted children is less satisfactory than the theory that they were gifted but unfulfilled all along. The heredity argument points in this direction. Further, although we know comparatively little about the brain, it seems unlikely that it should change its characteristics or its way of functioning because something suddenly 'clicks' after the passage of time, or because of a change in atmosphere or lessons.

d Gifted, but with blind spots

'Why can't he do maths?' is a concern sometimes expressed about a child who seems to do well at everything else. Blind spots seem more allowable when they occur in children who are intelligent but not outstanding. Where a gifted child is concerned, a blind spot seems almost perverse.

Granted that there is a general intellectual faculty that comprehensive IQ tests measure, it should follow that most normal achievements should lie well within the grasp of those who are shown to have a very high IQ. The presence of specific talents along with this general faculty does not really argue against the point, for these should be responsible for a gifted child excelling at one thing or another. They do not, so far as is known, crowd each other out. Verbal talent, musical talent, manipulative skill, artistic talent, are by no means mutually exclusive.

There are a few cases where some perceptual problem may tell against a gifted child in a particular subject. A tendency to see words the wrong way round has been mentioned in the case of Gerald, in Chapter 1. His difficulty with reading and writing probably stemmed from this, but was undoubtedly complicated by resistance to his teaching and to a natural inclination in his personality to pursue his interests in an individual, rather than an academic, way.

Visual or muscular oddities can obviously affect a gifted child's liking for and performance in activities requiring good eye and hand co-ordination. Athletics of certain kinds come to mind here, but they also can affect modelling and early work in science. Nature study has been known to prove unpleasant for young children with an allergy to certain plants or pollen; a child with mild hay fever may not realize why he will surprise a progressive teacher who believes in outdoor classes in summer by asking to be allowed back into the classroom to read.

Where a gifted child seems to have a blind spot it is always worth running one's mind over the possible physical reasons why he should be lagging behind in a particular subject. But the answer might be more psychological. There are many ways in which an emotional blockage may be set up which makes it difficult for a gifted child to come to terms with a subject. There are three main facets to such blockages.

The first concerns the nature of the teaching, the personality of the teacher, and the material used. If each of these is dull, most children may be put off the subject. Some case histories, however, suggest that a child of average intelligence may put up with more tedious repetition than a gifted child, before concentration evaporates in favour of day-dreaming. A gifted mind can be very intolerant of a learning situation that lacks stimulation, novelty or challenge. When he perceives at the start that the syllabus is of such a kind, he may not treat the subject seriously at all.

The second is a matter of pride. Gifted children often resent a bluff, 'wake-up-you-dozy-lot' manner that relies on irony to dramatize a point in the classroom. This is the epitome of the teacher-pupil relationship of, say, forty years ago. It persists, in varying degrees, and it must be admitted that many children thrive in these circumstances. The relationship which often works better with a gifted child (and which may be totally unsuitable for many in the same class) is that of two adults, one of whom has specialized knowledge which the other is anxious to find out about and discuss. In a school where a gifted child finds both situations, he may reserve his efforts for the more satisfying one. If, as a result, he has been once made to look a fool in the other situation, he may regard that subject as too disagreeable to persevere with, even with better teaching. This of course presents a dilemma to many teachers and will be discussed separately.

The third facet has nothing directly to do with teaching at all. Children have to live with other children whether they are gifted or not. It makes a point of contact with classmates, if one can say 'Gosh, I do find geometry impossible!' Someone who is uniformly successful at school seems rather unapproachable to the others. In extreme cases, a gifted child deliberately under-achieves across the board, in all activities, so that he does not become conspicuous and therefore suspect or alien to the rest.

There are other ways in which a gifted child can develop a 'blind spot'. In any event, this is more likely to be a result of his individual personality reacting to its environment, rather than an oddity of the brain itself.

*   *   *

None of the patterns of development described in this chapter presents an unanswerable problem for the theory that giftedness begins at birth and becomes apparent over time without undergoing drastic changes in the overall level of intelligence. The way in which giftedness becomes apparent varies according to the individual child's personality and what happens to him. The giftedness itself probably does not change. Meanwhile the particular talents that a child displays may indeed reflect differences in the kind of high intelligence that each gifted child has, although there is probably a very similar vein of overall basic ability which each shares at a high level.

The evidence on this last point is in conflict. But fewer assumptions about the nature of intellectual functions have to be made if the view expressed here is accepted. The alternative theory could be to maintain that different types of gifted child have altogether different types of brain power. It is easier to maintain that the brains themselves are very similar, but how they are used can vary considerably, according to inherited personality, upbringing and with whom a child learns to identify.

Four
Superior brain function

If we knew more about how an ordinary brain works we should be in a better position to decide what is special about a gifted child's brain power. No one really understands how it is that a small bag of complicated cell-arrangements can possibly perform all the functions of storing material to be memorized; deciding what objects round it need special attention; learning and recognizing associations between what is present and past; working out what needs to be done to change a bad situation into a better; learning to speak or sing; and how to direct the actions of hands and legs in complicated activities like sewing, dancing, or playing ice hockey or playing the piano. Analogies have been made comparing the brain with servo-mechanisms, analogue computers and even complex filtration plants, to aid this understanding. But most theories leave one feeling, 'Well, the brain must be more subtle than *that*.'

If, however, you set about observing human behaviour in a systematic way, using controlled experimental situations, you can draw conclusions about *what sort of tasks* the brain is likely to be performing, even if you have not answered the question of *how* it performs them.

Piaget, the great Swiss psychologist, realized a long time ago that if you do this to children at successive stages of their growth, and observe how they set about and succeed or fail with problems requiring different kinds of mental activity, you could list the new jobs that the brain learns to do as it develops, and as the child gains in experience. To be certain of accurate findings, he needed to conduct tests with a large number of children of varying ability, to observe their behaviour meticulously in each test, and to analyse the tests themselves with great care, before deciding exactly why it was that one should be more difficult than another. He found it useful to note what children said about the tests and about their efforts to solve them. This revealed the kind of mental blocks they met with when they got stuck.

Piaget's work has several points of contact with any study of gifted children. He was able to identify mental processes in the growth of intelligence, and it can be expected that these are things that gifted children are able to do *sooner* than others, and possibly in *an improved way*. These are not the same: 'sooner' implies that gifted children are always at later stages of Piaget's description of intellectual growth than other children of the same age; 'an improved way' suggests that when a gifted child is at the stage of 'classification', his brain can perform the tasks of classifying things in more ingenious ways than normal children at the same stage. Another way of drawing this distinction is to ask whether gifted children are simply accelerated in development, or whether they have equipment which leads them to perform at a superior level, whatever the tasks for their stage of development might be.

For a long time Piaget's kind of work was pursued on the Continent with little parallel effort elsewhere. Similarly, inquiries into IQ (what it means and how to measure it) went ahead in the UK and the USA particularly, with little cross-reference to what Piaget was finding. More recently, efforts have been made to link the two, as will be described later in this chapter.

When a child is starting to notice and recognize objects in

and around his cot—well within the first year of his life—
the first kinds of mental event were described by Piaget as
sensori-motor intelligence. This means getting an understanding
of what happens when you see something and reach for it,
touch it and push it: it moves, forwards or backwards,
according to what you do to it. During the first two years of his life,
a child is learning how he can affect what is around him, and
how he can be affected by things. He uses his senses
('sensori-') in order to get better control of his actions
('-motor'). Obviously, if this is called infantile intelligence,
then a measure of giftedness at this age must be the speed
with which a child masters straightforward things, like
picking up a ruler, which is hard for small fingers, as
opposed to a corner of a fluffy toy, which is much easier.
Few children at this stage are going to do anything intelligent with the ruler! But those who are getting mastery of this
kind and becoming less clumsy are developing a repertoire
which encourages more intellectual use of the mind—
because the child gains confidence about translating wishes
into acts.

It might be thought that this was athletic development as
opposed to, or even instead of, the growth of intelligence. It
is comparatively novel for people to accept that a natural
athlete and a gifted scholar may be one and the same child.
In infancy they probably are; later it may be that, in order to
concentrate on being one, the other identity will gradually
disappear. More likely, as time goes by, the child is led to
incline more towards sport or, according to the encouragement he gets from parents and his friends, to look at one
ability as desirable and the other as unsuitable 'for people
like us'. Countless schools have felt that it is only fair for
some to excel at scholarships and others to excel on the
football field. Many perpetuate the myth of exclusive categories by discouraging what they discern as scholarship

material from wasting too much time out of doors, and implying to sports heroes that they have a separate route whereby they might just scrape an 'O' level or two. Times and thought are changing, but the myth dies hard, especially for boys. Curiously, it is less true for girls. One answer may lie in the fact that professional games-playing is an aim in life with strong appeal for many boys but few girls; another that books about boys' school life tend to contrast the athlete and the swot, while girls' school stories allow the same girl to be clever at her studies *and* naughty, *and* good at music, *and* good at tennis or horse riding.

In the child's second year some start is made towards *pre-conceptual thought*. This stage is mainly characteristic between two and four years, but its seeds can be discovered in a toddler's behaviour before that. This kind of 'thinking' involves use of memory, and observation of relations between objects in order to get at them or move them. Piaget observed children in cots where a pulley arrangement had been rigged up to permit them to tug at a lever and draw a coloured ball towards them. Early in life, the pulley is one thing to a child and the ball another. Pulling the one and getting the other might as well be fortuitous until the child registers that it is a case of cause and effect. It is hard for somebody at this stage of thought to apply the principle of 'lever-pulley-ball' to anything else, unless it is carefully demonstrated for him. Generalization, or expecting that other levers and pulleys (or objects like them) might have the same function, is beyond him, but if he is shown a ball in the same place as in the test while lying in a cot without a pulley arrangement, he may look as if he is searching for a lever.

Treating preconceptual thought at its simplest, it is worth

considering the difference between a young toddler and an older toddler when in a strange room for the first time. The younger one knows what certain doors look like at home and where they lead to. But he may well 'miss' a door, especially a closed door, if he has not been shown its use before. If he doesn't feel comfortable, cannot attract his mother and doesn't know how to get out of the situation, he probably sits down and howls. An older child may feel more like exploring anyway. But if he is bored or uncomfortable, he certainly knows what a door looks like. Brass-knobbed or plastic-handled, his experience tells him they are much the same and that they are useful as exits.

A gifted toddler seems often more composed because he has built up a repertoire of activity like turning door-handles, which have a satisfactory effect in different circumstances. He is probably generalizing from his experience much more as well as benefiting from his better co-ordination, which helps him to get what he wants.

We can hypothesize, too, that he may have a better understanding with his parents, particularly his mother. This may be because both are more intelligent, and more sensitive to each other's hints. If he is confident that he can talk, grunt, nudge, or simply look in such a way that he is understood by his mother, he gains immeasurably in confidence. This is true of any child, as is shown in studies of premature separation from a mother. But, for the reasons suggested, it is likely to be *more true* of a gifted child. Being more confident, he explores more, and gives himself more experiences on which to build.

Piaget reckoned that at four years of age a child ought to be starting to demonstrate *intuitive thought*. This means that he can obey more orders, without being shown how; the reason is that he has begun to *visualize* what is involved in carrying them out, before having the necessary equipment in his hand. 'Take a glass from the kitchen, fill it with milk, and bring it to me, please,' you can ask him. If he knows where the kitchen is, and in which cupboard the glasses are kept, he can see himself doing what is required. The milk may pose a problem, if he has never extracted a bottle from the fridge, prised off the seal, or poured milk from it into a glass. This is a complex series of motions, once it is broken down into separate acts. A child is not like an adult stranger in a house: he cannot 'imagine' where the milk might be, nor can he draw on experience of many different encounters with bottles, bottle tops and metal foil, to suggest to him how he might best broach the milk itself. If one part of the sequence is a puzzle, the rest of the order may get muddled or forgotten. A child is not dissimilar to an adult over this: as soon as the mission becomes threatening to self-esteem it is resented, and the true details of it are lost to the conscious mind. 'Now—what on earth was it you wanted me to do?' is a frequent adult reaction to this experience.

It should be noted that confidence about basic sensorimotor control, and about using memory to fix things in time and space, are prerequisites for doing the tasks of the 'intuitive thought' period well. A gifted child, we may suppose, who is good at such tasks at an early age, must be happy with his hands, his eye and his memory of what goes where. But he is probably capable of retrieving more easily than most those bits of memory that are relevant to the problem in front of him. He needs to store facts, but this is useless without a competent and confident retrieval system. He may possibly be better both at storing and retrieving; not enough is known about memory for us to be sure whether this is more likely or that he is simply more sophisticated about using what he learns.

The parents of a gifted child of about this age often note

for the first time that 'he seems to have a very good memory'. For 'good memory' to be apparent, however, probably depends a great deal on successful negotiation of the stages leading up to intuitive thought.

No child of this age is really proficient at planning how to cope with problems involving objects he has not met, or been shown how to use. Similarly, it is very difficult for a child to remain logical and single-minded about known objects when they suddenly appear in different positions or shapes. What is taller, is usually 'bigger' to a five-year-old, even if he has seen a tall shape made out of a small amount of plasticine, and put next to a large amount squashed into a pancake. If he puts the same amounts of water, from the same cup, first into an empty goldfish bowl and then into a thin vase, he may very well declare that there is more water in the goldfish bowl. Part of this failure to preserve what is called the 'constancy of volume' of objects is a matter of semantics: we can never be certain how far 'taller' and 'bigger' mean the same thing to a young child, or whether they necessarily mean the same thing to him in different contexts. But, typically, he will for a number of years have problems about recognizing objects as being the same or having the same characteristics when the perceptual cues are changed.

Piaget considered that the concept of volume starts to become properly established at seven, but that it is only perfected at about age eleven. Work by two British psychologists, Lovell and Shields, showed that gifted children are consistently better than other children at constancy problems. But they also found that gifted children vary a great deal among themselves over this. It is therefore a likely, but not an invariable, characteristic of a gifted child that he will show a better understanding of the nature of the things around him; that he will recognize them when they reappear in different forms; and that he will note how they can change in certain conditions.

Concrete operations is the term Piaget gave to the next phase of development. This covers the age bracket seven to eleven. The most obvious difference that this involves in a child's thinking is the increase in the range of operations that lie within his scope.

He will understand more complicated orders, and he will carry them out more accurately. In doing so he will fit together the things that he knows in ways that do not require special prompting. In an earlier example a young child was asked to go and pour out a glass of milk. An intelligent girl of seven or eight can follow a simple recipe from a children's cookery book, and will search for appropriate ingredients, make measurements and use the kitchen equipment that she needs. If she has watched her mother or helped with parts of a meal, like making salad dressings, she is less likely to make mistakes. But she has got to the point of being able to work out from a set of instructions what is required and put it into practice.

No sensible child will avoid asking advice (unless his pride is deeply concerned with preserving independence), but advice is not a crucial part of the proceedings. This is partly because the principles of 'constancy' are being understood. Not perfectly perhaps, but increasingly better. 'Boil for five minutes' in the recipe is referring to the same five minutes that a girl can observe passing on the kitchen clock, as the big hand moves from eleven to twelve. The salt in the salt cellars is the same as that in the round drum in the pantry, only there is less of it. But plain flour is always different from self-raising; they appear in different coloured packs. She can therefore work out a concrete operation on her own, using what she knows to draw straightforward inferences.

Gifted children's personalities influence the kind of operations they favour, irrespective of the level of reasoning power they have reached. This makes it difficult to discern exactly how they are accelerating during this particular phase. More research by Lovell and Shields, comparing a sample of gifted children between the ages of eight and a half and eleven and a half with work done by an unselected sample of rather older children, pointed to the conclusion that a gifted child is likely to be able to cope with the concrete operations thought processes that were required for Piaget's tests, at an *earlier* age than most. But two gifted children let loose in a kitchen for an afternoon might achieve entirely different results.

Anna is nine. She has an IQ of 140 (Stanford Binet). Some of her greatest pleasures come from making things with her fingers—whether this be embroidery, modelling, painting or cooking. Playing the piano might also qualify in this category: she is musically gifted as well. She is neat and precise in her work, and likes taking adult performance as a standard at which to aim. Frequently this makes her too ambitious and leads her into time problems. But she has very intense concentration, which blinds her completely to her brothers' interruptions and she usually, therefore, ends up with something that she can be proud of and show around. Another important characteristic in this context is her desire to be from time to time an active organizer of the household, after the manner of her mother and the au pair. She sometimes makes you feel she would like to take over the running of the house entirely for a few days.

One evening when I was interviewing her parents Anna surprised them by saying she would prepare supper. Her mother was slightly alarmed and her father suspicious, but fortunately they gave her her head. 'What are you going to do?' her mother asked. 'I'm going to find something nice in my cookery book,' Anna answered, settling down solemnly with a copy of 'My Learn to Cook Book'. She asked some questions like 'Have we got any parsley?' and adjusted her plans accordingly. Eventually, she disappeared into the kitchen, where she did not appear to notice my face at the dining-room hatch as I watched. She hard-boiled some eggs (one for each person having the meal), peeled them, cut off the tops and scooped out the yolks, beat these up with a small mixture of oil, vinegar, mustard and black pepper, refilled the eggs and up-ended them, so that they 'stood' on their flat ends, and finally decorated them with tomato strips and pieces of parsley, to make faces and hats. This last effort was rather too finicky for her, as she was tired, and she enlisted her mother's help. She was pleased at being complimented, but accepted her father's mild criticism that there was a bit too much pepper in a very objective way, as though noting it for next time. 'It should have said "a small pinch" in the recipe,' she commented.

Karen is also gifted, and only slightly younger than Anna. Her parents do not encourage her to do a great deal in the kitchen. She has asked, and has been allowed to make things like jam tarts and fairy cakes. Her approach is very individual, however, and although she gets a kick out of it herself, no one actually benefits.

When confronted by instructions and ingredients, Karen thinks in terms of a challenge to her ingenuity. She has tried to bake fairy cakes with a dollop of jam in the middle; to make scones out of dough pressed down and flattened into shapes like elephants; to make a new kind of salad, including plenty of grass, and chunks of unbaked potato.

This is not because she is unintelligent. It is how her personality and her humour incline her to use her intelligence.

Anna wants to be like her mother, an efficient provider,

who pleases everyone with what she produces in the kitchen. She wants to act independently. Getting answers right is important to her, as are compliments, and seeing people enjoy what she has done.

Karen doesn't attach much importance, if any, to stepping into her mother's shoes from time to time. She enjoys compliments, but she enjoys surprising and even shocking her family too: sets of instructions are only starting-off points and her own ideas seem every bit as interesting as repeating what countless other cooks have done. But *experiment*—that's different! How splendid to try to produce something original. If it doesn't work, there may be a good laugh in it, anyway.

This contrast has been drawn with the benefit of knowing more about the girls than just their culinary traits. The point is that at this age it can be very difficult to see how well the 'concrete operations' have been working. A child who fits neatly into the pattern, like Anna, could almost have grown up under Piaget's influence. Not so Karen. And yet a number of the comments she makes as she prepares a witch's brew suggest that a very lively mind is at work (e.g. on grass in salad: 'It must be good for you, because it's the only thing cows eat and we get milk from them'). She is probably following her own logic; the problem is, that it is not easily analysed or understood.

From about the age of eleven onwards the stage of *formal operations* begins. The simplest way to take this is to note a transition from making plans and carrying them out, to working out what would happen if a particular plan *were* carried out. The child thinking at this level can handle hypothetical data, work out a possible cause and effect, and construct a test adequate to show whether his idea was right or not, or *how* right it was.

The kind of test that Piaget devised, which allows a child to demonstrate he has reached formal operational thinking, presents a challenge to most adults. This is reasonable, given that Piaget visualized people getting better and better at it, and applying it in more subtle ways, rather than moving on to a further, more rarefied type of thinking altogether.

He showed children an apparatus consisting of a pendulum suspended from a bar. The rate of the swing of the pendulum could depend on the height of the bar from the ground, the weight on the end of the pendulum, the length of the connection between pendulum and bar, and on the strength with which the pendulum was pushed. All were adjustable. The test was to devise a means of changing the swing from one rate to another.

Adroit thinking at this level means working out a scheme in one's mind to test which combination of factors, involving what level of change, would have the desired effect. It is then a question of putting the test into action, noting the results, and working out further tests in logical sequence (assuming one hasn't had the supreme luck to get everything right first time).

It has been shown that this level of thinking is not entirely foreign to some gifted children who are markedly younger. It is possible, for example, to see an element of this in Anna's cooking plans (see above) particularly where she asked speculatively whether there was any parsley, and combined the answer with other factors she carried in her head, to work out which recipe to choose. The same research has also suggested that most eleven-year-olds are still unprepared for this sort of test.

Some gifted children do not perform well at Piaget's tests. Possibly laboratory replications of them are too rigidly applied. His work on mental processes may, however, miss out something which helps the gifted child to demonstrate a good IQ result. But the tests are also at a tangent, perhaps, to some of the more imaginative thinking of children who are creatively gifted. Piaget's work is essentially dealing with stages of rational thought.

Five
Gifted creativity

To be creative it is not necessary to be gifted. I am going to use creativity in a restricted sense, as suggested in the first chapter. This is to accept the argument that there are some children with a high IQ—but not a gifted IQ—who are particularly creative, and deserve the label 'gifted'. The kind of expression that their creativity takes may vary from scientific exploration to feats of imaginative writing and artistic production. Or, it may be a kind of free-floating originality, a fund of ideas that are not or cannot be put into practice, because the child has not yet found the right medium for them. (One example was neatly described by his headmaster thus: 'Gerald is always threatening to be creative'.)

It is quite possible that some children may have gifted creativity ascribed to them, when they simply have an exceptional skill with a particular instrument, or at representational drawing. Later they may disappoint. This is why the word 'artistic' is used above. This concept transcends technical flair, although they will need technique of some kind, at some stage, to bear any recognizable fruit. In the kind of creativity I am trying to describe, there must be the promise of extending the range of what surprises or delights us, not simply reproduction.

It is generally easier for people, including research workers, to agree on what is not creative than what is. The same applies to the question of what kind of brainwork is involved. Meticulous pursuit of other people's thoughts, however precise and clever, does not strike one as creative. But whether or not the workings of a critic's mind are looked on as creative—given that he is not simply analysing and reproducing thoughts, but is working out connections between them and presenting their central ideas in a fresh light—is simply a matter of opinion. Is the critic's brain less creative than the artist's? Does a young child who reads a poem, understands it with difficulty, and then talks intelligently about it, give less promise of 'creativity' than one who enjoys making unusual collages, the wilder the better?

All this is by way of saying that most people have an idea of what 'creativity' is, and each could describe it in terms that others understand, but do not necessarily accept. However imprecise—because there are real children with real prospects involved in it and not just an academic conflict—the concept is worth discussing.

Some experts believe that a creative genius must have mental equipment that is in most respects very similar to the very high IQ group. All the same, you cannot pick out artists and Nobel prize-winners simply by looking at IQ. Others will argue that the differences between the ways in which the 'creative' and the 'high IQ' groups think are greater than the similarities. But are these really differences in thought, or in personality?

This is not the book in which to examine these arguments exhaustively. They are not likely to be resolved conclusively anyway. But it is worth considering what the mind of a young creative genius might be like. It may help in getting him recognized for what he is, particularly as he is more likely to be ignored or over-disciplined, and frustrated, than the high IQ child who conforms to what his teachers require of him. It might also provide pointers for educating such children. They seem to respond to different kinds of teaching methods, to different subjects, to different teachers. Possibly more of these pointers will be negative than positive: that is, a study of their mentality may suggest more about how their creativity may be stifled than about how it may be fed. This is because, of its nature, creativity needs to surprise. Telling a person to surprise you must be self-defeating.

One major battle-ground has been the relation to creativity of the difference between 'convergers' and 'divergers', mentioned briefly in the first chapter. It is not enough to say that a more creative child will tend to be divergent (i.e. performs well at 'open ended' tests where there is no single right answer) rather than convergent (i.e. performs better at fully structured tests where marks are gained only for correct answers). In fact, Liam Hudson, who has been responsible for much of the research in this area, regards the issue of creativity as only 'tangential' to convergence-divergence.

Certainly some of the characteristics observed in young divergers seem to suggest that they 'diverge' in the sense of personality rather than in forming thoughts or associations. In short, these children have been shown as:

a interested in rarities and oddities.
b having a broader range of interests, especially outside school.
c interested in reading, current affairs etc. rather than in standard school activities.
d more expressive in their emotions (whether real or affected).
e more likely to let their feelings colour their work.
f less likely to accept recommendations or beliefs on trust.
g less concerned about agreeing with the majority view.
h more tolerant and 'liberal' (although not when this is in conflict with their own desires).

Most of these descriptions (which have been established by research) are the kind that would be used of a child who is simply more flexible and less responsive to outside influence. This is a character type that runs in families. Common experience suggests that rigid, authoritarian families are unlikely to have children of this kind; that homes where the parents are easy on discipline, and sceptical about what their neighbours or what 'experts' say, are more likely to have these children. Some research, in fact, does show that divergent parents tend to have divergent children. Of course children often rebel against the parents' attitudes and way of life. This merely raises a question of upbringing, suggesting that all gifted children, whether convergers or divergers, have similar thought apparatus. It is the tuning that is different, and this has little to do with the children themselves. But this seems more acceptable if one is talking about all children, than about very intelligent children. Some kind of mental flair may be released by a liberal upbringing, in their case, which may not happen with just any child. What kind of mental flair would this be?

The open-ended tests used by Getzels and Jackson, who were among the first to suggest ways of identifying what they called the 'high creative' as opposed to the 'high IQ' child, can be regarded as giving a chance for an intelligent child to show four aspects of creative work:

1. Originality
2. Fluidity
3. Flexibility
4. Elaboration

In a typical test, a child might be asked to write down as many uses as possible for a commonplace object such as a bucket or a clothes peg. Scoring the test is much more a question of 'getting the feel of the data' than following fixed principles that allow standard quantification. Some unkind critics have pointed out that the tester needs all four of the above aspects, in good measure, to make his assessments. Two children may produce the same number of suggestions for using a bucket but be awarded entirely different markings for creativity:

Roger (age nine)		*Rupert* (age nine)
i for carrying: water		i for making butter
ii	milk	ii for growing strawberries in
iii	cocoa	
iv	beer	iii as a helmet
v	wine	iv firewood
vi	other liquid	v for trapping wasps (you put jam in the bottom, and cover over most of the top)
vii for measuring things		vi with flowers, a lady's hat for Easter Parade
		vii for making sandcastles

Roger may have the higher IQ. But he does seem comparatively dull, doesn't he? Talking to him afterwards, he may well say something like, 'Well, you *wouldn't* really use a bucket for carrying *food*, would you?' It had crossed his mind, only to be dismissed. Confronted with some of the items in Rupert's list, he politely admires the ingenuity of some of the items. But many seem to him 'rather silly'. Either they are 'not the sort of thing you would do, really—chopping up a bucket for firewood seems very wasteful', or they do not strike him as the kind of replies one ought to be giving in a serious test. A test is rather a serious business for Roger, although he enjoys them in his way. That is partly why he has a high IQ. He does not enjoy open-ended tests so much, because of a feeling that it is not entirely clear how he is expected to tackle them and do well at them. Some of his preference for concrete tasks and objectivity comes out in his one unusual suggestion 'for measuring things'.

Rupert need not be an extrovert with a chip. But he is inclined to be rather critical of the test, for he instinctively queries the premise behind most tests. This one at least avoids the need to try to be painstakingly accurate over detail that he finds more tedious than Roger. It also gives an opportunity for surprising the tester, or 'sending up' the test. Talking to him, afterwards, he may reveal something akin to the concept, 'Wonder what they'll make of that!' or 'Now they'll have to think of some different questions!' Shown Roger's answers, he may say something like 'I suppose that's the kind of answers they really wanted.' But he will defend his ideas. They are original, in that he tends to have chosen uses that others have not thought of. They emerge in a fluid way: another boy might have some original ideas, but be restricted to one or two. Rupert moves from one kind of idea to another, in a very flexible way. (Contrast Roger's catalogue of 'bucketable' liquids.) He is also interested in presenting his ideas, as opposed to simply stating them: this makes him elaborate some of them, for example in explaining the wasp trap. Some tests are better suited to providing evidence about fluidity and elaboration.

All this sounds as if it depends on writing. Roger is probably the more conscientious writer. In fact, some of the more unsystematic and more original creative children may well find their originality outstripping their writing ability. A personal interview, in which questions can be answered orally, must be easier for younger children. It is an attractive idea in that it offers the opportunity of judging the 'real' creative-sounding answers, which ought to tell us more about the 'creativity' so revealed. This is perfectly true. But the drawback is that most children can be made more 'creative' simply by having a sympathetic tester giving the right kind of encouragement in his questions. If Roger had had such a personal interview—with the tester putting an inflection on 'How many different uses of a bucket can you think of?', then he would have been motivated to declare some ideas that he had filtered out as perhaps 'silly'. Roger will oblige any teacher, within reason. Rupert is more selective.

These considerations prompt one to suggest two other ways in which the 'creative' mind might be different:

a It is more dependent on a satisfactory atmosphere and suitable stimulation to be productive or to communicate.

b It needs a personal wavelength, or a sense that a particular person is listening, for it to find a 'satisfactory atmosphere'.

These points are observed tendencies rather than established fact. They presuppose, of course, that the work of Getzels and Jackson, and that of others who have followed them, has got at least something to do with 'creativity'. They are important in a practical sense, because they have implications for the kind of educational situation in which creatively gifted children might be expected to shine, and from which they might benefit.

Further comparison of Roger and Rupert suggests two other related differences between them:

a Roger is filtering out the kind of response that seems to him to be 'not the right thing'. Rupert presents his ideas with little censorship of this kind.

b Roger is thorough in pursuing a line of thought he believes to be right and relentlessly so, as in his catalogue of liquids. Rupert is less thorough; he elaborates, but he does not catalogue.

These are contrasts which can be viewed as representing dependence on different kinds of mental process, or preference for producing different kinds of effect on the people around them. These are not necessarily alternatives: mentality and personality are interwoven, rather like a chicken-and-egg problem. But some have noted that a case can be made out that *forgetting* has a crucial function to fulfil in making somebody more 'creative'.

This sounds paradoxical. Surely a creative person is adept at producing new ideas, for which there must be raw material in the form of memories?

But the point is a fair one that complete recall—whether of series, solutions or questions—is counter-productive where *new* ideas are concerned. Roger, for all his giftedness, is the slave of his memory when his tedious catalogue of suitable liquids for a bucket is developed. In another context, where a new solution to a problem is required, Roger's thinking might also be closely tied to what his memory dictates. That is, he might run over all the associations he has with the objects involved, and all the ways he knows of tackling similar problems. Faced by a river, and the need to get across, he will consider the possibility of bridges, stepping-stones, shallows that can be forded and boats. Finding none he might be stumped, although being very intelligent he might gradually work through less likely associations as well, and perhaps hit upon an answer.

Rupert in the same situation might be more creative. Of course, he would probably start by querying whether he really needed to cross the river *at all*. Creative solutions, whether they are in a military, an industrial, an entertainment or any area, are often rooted in intelligent speculation about the premise on which everything is based. For example: 'Do we really need to take control of a large natural harbour when we land in France on D-Day?' (the result was Mulberry, the artificial harbour) ; 'Why should rubber trees only grow by the Amazon?'; 'Why shouldn't serious social issues be examined on the stage?', etc.

Rupert will also think of the practical solutions that Roger suggested, but he will put up some ideas that, typically, break some of the implicit rules in the way the question is set. For instance, he may propose a tunnel under the river, partly because this does not represent exactly what most people mean by 'across'. He will not filter out the more eccentric schemes that occur to him, because of their surprise value when he announces them, and also because he is not totally wedded to the ideal of a practical outcome. Sometimes he may prefer a 'poetic' solution, that appeals to humour or aesthetics, and that is calculated to irritate the hatchet-faced pragmatist. He may suggest sending to a local zoo for a team of elephants to ferry them across. In certain circumstances, this might (just) prove to be not only practical but also the most efficient means; yet Roger would not suggest or approve of it because it might be or might seem 'silly'.

It is not an unreasonable theory that the comparative unpopularity of Rupert (depending on home, school, etc.) may be due not so much to the apparent silliness of his ideas, but to the fact that they sometimes work. Coming from somebody whose attitude seems 'wrong', or questioning, success is scarcely tolerable.

A very strong 'creative' child, then, as opposed to a very strong 'IQ' child, may have a mind that conveniently forgets:

a order: what follows what, in sequence or hierarchy.
b the 'correct' way of doing things.
c the need to avoid embarrassment (for himself or for others).

74

What he does *not* forget (and this must be a large part of his gift) are associations between people, objects and ideas. He can summon these to the surface of his mind, in a form in which they can be examined and discussed, more easily than others.

Computer analogies with the brain can be more misleading than helpful, because they oversimplify. But this one may be justified. Both types of gifted child may have a superior data storing system: superior in terms of the amount of information that can be handled at once, the categorization of what gets stored, and the data retrieval system. But the high IQ child's use of that system is controlled and precise; some would say that it is inhibited from bringing to light many of its more unusual associations, which would be food for the creative child's innovation. Others would point to the sense of goal-direction and practical application in the way the high IQ child retrieves his data. He certainly appeals as a safer companion to cross the river with, though perhaps a less entertaining one.

Teachers who have had excellent scholars pass their way sometimes comment on 'the brilliant all-rounder'. He or she occurs rarely. Head teachers of some famous schools have told me they might get one, sometimes two, in a good year. These seem to transcend the idea of 'high IQ' and 'creative', because they are outstanding at everything they touch. They produce the most precise accounts of physics experiments, and the most imaginative essays. They excel at team games as well as at individual sports. The distinctions drawn between Roger's and Rupert's mental processes do not seem to apply in their case. They seem to be able to switch from one way of approaching a problem to another—whether it involves learning, reproducing, or making something new—without apparent effort or lessening of success.

Why? To say they have a 'superbrain' says nothing. An

economic theory is that they are naturally in sympathy with the problems they are set and the people who set them. Therefore they do not need to filter out 'silly' thoughts, and yet they can apply themselves rigorously to a repetitive task which demands painstaking precision. They can still have their preferences, and they can still be bored. But they have not developed *blockages* against performances. Their mental equipment may be the same as that of other gifted children. But their high motivation in all fields argues a gift of confidence that must relate back to early encouragement at home to take on anything, and enthusiasm for appreciation at nursery school and junior school, by other children as much as by teachers. These 'brilliant all-rounders' are often described as being very popular. Success with other children breeds success; it may be that early experiences of dealing with other children are important in establishing a level platform of confidence from which the gifted can feel assured about tackling any kind of problem. The US term 'socially gifted' seems very apt for them.

It is interesting to note in this context that Liam Hudson found a sharper distinction between arts and science specialists in Great Britain than was found in the USA, in terms of convergence-divergence. (The British children taking science tended to be convergers, and those taking arts subjects, divergers.) One possible implication is that in Great Britain there is more insistence on doing things in particular ways, especially where science is concerned. This may affect other subjects too, but the gleam of hope for the diverger is the possibility of playing with heretical attitudes. This is easier in English and history, and easier still in fine arts or drama. Possibly we tend to polarize our children (*even our gifted children*) at very early stages, at home and at their first schools. It is this which may make the 'brilliant all-rounders' such a rare breed, and it is the same thing which may exaggerate the impression that a 'high IQ' and a 'high creative' child must have very different kinds of superior brain.

If this is so, the logical policy of parents and schools should be to maximize the opportunity for a gifted child to develop interests across a wide front. This may have a negative rather than a positive implication: i.e. he or she should not be given to understand that such and such an interest is inferior or wrong, rather than enforcing a wide curriculum which may restrict development of personal skills or preferred activities.

Six
Problems when young

It is still fairly common to hear educationists and teachers contend that a gifted child needs no special provision because his superior intelligence must see him through. In 1973 a spokesman for a local authority made this comment to me when I asked him whether there were any services recommended by his education department for gifted children:

> Gifted children—if they exist, that is, and I suppose they do to some extent—gifted children aren't a problem exactly. We've got lots of problems—we've got some kids who ought to be in an ESN school but aren't, we've got truancy, we've got a couple of real 'jungles'. In the older lot, we've got gangs and too few teachers. There's a hell of a lot to work at without taking on extra responsibilities. No, a gifted child—he's going to do very well. If he's ahead of the class he can always read on his own. And sometimes you get an opportunity to use them as teachers you know, they help the slower ones along. Teachers need a bit of help, what with the size of classes. . . . We *have* had a kiddie or two who's been getting on badly and the head teacher's got them seen by the psychologist. They turned out to be much brighter than anyone had thought—I don't know about *gifted*. Well, they seem to be getting on better now. But any teacher can make mistakes.

He went on to talk about the work that he and his colleagues put in to further the ideal of providing every child in the district with an equal chance of good education. Admittedly, circumstances (lack of funds, antiquated buildings, staff turnover, etc.) were very much against everyone receiving a good chance to get 'O' and 'A' levels, and to go on to further education. But the figures on 'A' levels were good for the local state schools and were slowly getting better. Based on the principle of fair shares for all and provided the government could be persuaded to invest more, they were sure to build schools and pay teachers more, which would be for the good of the whole community.

This was the real struggle, as far as he was concerned. The possible needs (hypothetical, to him) of a specialized category were well down the list of priorities. Higher up the list came provision of kindergarten or nursery school education, which was greatly lacking and which he recognized as likely to make up for some of the head start which he understood that children in better-off families had when it came to developing an early curiosity and liking for learning. This is mentioned because it may be one of the means by which young gifted children from poorer homes, or from homes where learning is disregarded, may be spotted for what they are, and helped.

At a very early age it is possible that all children who are gifted will escape notice of everybody who, as a parent or a relative, has not actually got an eye out for comparing potential. A toddler is a toddler, and will be loved for his toddler characteristics, whether he is gifted or not. Later he may seem more difficult to get on with, as his independence and his attempts at older behaviour become more obvious. Because he cannot become adult and mature in his reactions all at once, there may be a difficult stage during which he seems to his parents to be impossible to understand, and perverse if not actually badly behaved. A child of five who is very gifted may have a mental age of eight, and perhaps a reading age of even eleven. But his emotional age may be stuck at around five. It may even be *less* than five, especially if he has had difficulties in getting on with his parents. This distinction between being intellectually advanced and slow to mature in terms of being frightened easily, or bursting into tears and tantrums when thwarted, is very important. It is usually at the root of the problem when a child like this is referred to a psychologist because 'he seems to be such a puzzle'.

Ian can write remarkably well for his age. He is five and a half. Here is a recent composition of his:

Yesterday I went to my Godmothers house and Daddy drove round the new roundabout at Richmond. He overtook 15 cars. One car was a red sports car. At my Godmothers there was a boy and a girl. The boy is Jonathan and I dont know the name of the girl. Jonathan was nauty with the raspberries. You must not pick the raspberries.

The spelling is his, except for the first 'raspberries'. Here it is obvious from the scratches on his diary exercise book that he got into trouble and asked for help. The second 'raspberries' he copied out carefully.,

Comparison of Ian's diary entry with those of his classmates shows that he produces twice the length; more complex words and ideas; less repetitive detail; original story lines which he generally follows through. He is in love with what he is doing. If he thinks of something interesting to say, he works out carefully how to put it down, and makes few mistakes. He thrives on compliments, too, and on the feeling that he is more successful than the others. When he talks he seems as confident as his writing sounds.

One class above him is James, who is nearly seven. On an IQ test, James proved that his intelligence was about as high as Ian's, allowing for the difference in age. But a page from James's diary reads: 'It was rening al day.'

This is a typical example of his output when he has not actually been urged by his teacher to step up production. He has no interest in writing, and repeats the same spelling mistakes over and over.

In other work, the gap between the two boys is less marked. But in reading, number work and nature study, it would be hard for an observer not to conclude that Ian was gifted, and James a bit dull. To be honest, James comes to life rather more in his classroom project on transport, where he has recently been working hard and ingeniously designing a bicycle taxi system to serve his town. This apart, his interest and his achievement are low.

James ducks out of contact with his teacher. He expects to be told that he has more to do, or that what he has done is wrong. He accepts comments of this kind good-naturedly, shakes his head, and gives a half-smile to his friends in the class as if to say, 'Well, that's school life all over, isn't it . . .'

He enjoys the company of these friends very much, although he is rarely the centre of attention. They take him for one of themselves, but are suggesting ideas or exploits to him far more than receiving them from him. A lot of the time he remains at the edge of their circle, drinking in their scene, but contributing little. He won't hold his own in arguments with them as a rule, even if he is sure he is right. In their eyes it is hard to see what role he fulfils, except that he admires them, refrains from complaining about anything to the teachers and plays a moderate game of football.

It might have been perfectly possible for James to continue his way through the state school system without disturbance.

His teachers had very little reason to suspect he should be capable of more. At times, during his first term at school, he did something—a drawing or a model—that put him in the front rank for attention. But he never stayed there long. Then a student teacher doing a project was allowed to put the boys of his form through part of an intelligence test. Most of the results followed the form teacher's expectations, except in James's case, where he performed remarkably well (fortunately it was a non-verbal test). When an educational psychologist was visiting the school, he was asked to talk to James; a request was later put to James's parents to have his IQ formally tested.

The teacher still finds it rather difficult to believe. It is not easy to get through to James. In fact, he has not been doing much better over the past four months, since the test. There are twenty-six in the class, and it is all too easy for him to sink into the background. 'You can't say to him—"Buck up, you're more intelligent than you pretend to be"—can you!' the form teacher told me. He has tried getting James to talk about what he likes, and what impresses him, to get an idea about how to stimulate him to try a new line, to learn more and to contribute more. But he has twenty-five others in his class.

James does not respond well to formal teaching. The transport project (where he suddenly decided that bicycle taxis were at first a funny idea, then worth describing in detail) managed to win his interest. This may have been because the other boys and girls were almost uniformly taken up by it too. It was not a solution where one child can look over another's work and say, loudly and complainingly, 'Look! Marjorie's writing tons!' James seems to need to be one of the gang very badly, and will not pursue something if they lose interest in it or disapprove of it.

Parkyn, who did a great deal of research on gifted children, asserted that the biggest difference between them and the other children he studied was in their voracious appetite for reading. James does not seem to share this. He uses the school library less often than the others, although he can read above the standard of his age group, and despite attempts to talk about books to him.

A visit to James's home gives some clues to why this should be. He had been living for almost a year with his great-aunt. His father stays there off and on, but James does not see much of him. His mother, who is divorced but has access, takes him out about once a month. The great-aunt also has two older children, of seventeen and fifteen, living with her. They have not got a great deal of time for James, although they have taken him to watch football. The great-aunt is very warm-hearted, and her house seems very happy. There are always visitors, and she regarded my visit as a perfectly ordinary event.

She is fifty, and has a strong belief that everybody, children included, should be left alone to do things in their own way. She hates the thought of pressure of any kind, particularly where education is concerned. Her own boys have emerged from their school (one is leaving this term) with an 'O' level apiece, and a strong disinclination to have anything to do with further education. They are both keen on stripping down motorbikes; they may be good at it, but this is difficult to tell. This is the first of their passions, the others being girls, football and pop music, in roughly that order. The older one works at a garage on an irregular basis. The second has a lot of vague plans like going on the road, or joining a commune in Amsterdam. Nobody in the house has any need or wish to read anything more difficult than a magazine with stories and pictures. The television set is on most of the time, for anyone passing by it to stop and watch if they feel like it.

Everyone is kind to James, including his father, although he is not often there while James is awake. But nobody has talked to him much. And nobody has stimulated him to have stronger curiosity about the world, to want to know how things work or to feel that he can share ideas with them and use words in the way they do. Nobody took much notice of what he was doing at school. It was presumed, in the comments made to him, that he must find school a bore, as they had all done.

His great-aunt was not at all surprised to be told by the school that James was very intelligent. 'Oh, he's a bright one, all right,' she commented. He was good at reminding her to water the houseplants, and he was quick at picking up a form of double patience which she liked. There is no question that she has given James a great deal of love and that he has been happy with her. That, in his life, is probably the most important feature she could have provided. But she can provide no incentive for him to develop his intellectual capacity. It simply is not in her nature. When asked about whether she or his father had any plans for his education, her comment was, 'I don't believe in making a fuss about schools. He goes to school, so let them get on with it.'

Her view that 'doing well at school doesn't mean doing well in life' is a fair argument against pressure, and against 'the academic rat race'. But she carries this to extremes when she pours scorn on 'bookworms'. If James is going to become interested in using his gifts, it will be through somebody at school attracting his attention and inspiring him with confidence and pleasure in work. Alternatively his father may concern himself more closely with him, although there is little sign of that at the moment.

The contrast with Ian's home life is very revealing. For one thing, Ian's mother has made regular contact with the school. His father likes to know what Ian is doing, and talks to him about it. Both discuss the problems of choosing the right school for him to go on to. This must have two very important effects. First, Ian has realized for a long time that his parents value talking with him, enjoy sharing his concerns, his interests and his triumphs and feel that education, in its broadest sense, is a good thing. Secondly, it means that Ian's teachers know a good deal more about him than other children whose parents do not make a habit of stopping by and talking about this and that. His form teacher admits this. Even a teacher who is determined not to have favourites, or to pay more attention to one child than another, must have a better understanding of a child whom he (or she) finds himself talking about more. It is inescapable. The better a child is known, the better the communication with him, and the better the understanding of his reactions when he is shown something new, or faced with something puzzling. He will be easier to teach then, in many ways (although possibly more demanding), and to most teachers he will be a more interesting and rewarding pupil.

The report on a follow-up study of a large number of children throughout Great Britain ('From Birth to Seven') showed conclusively that parents' interest in schooling and the number of visits they made were major factors contributing to success in primary school. There is no reason why this general rule should not apply to gifted children as well as to others.

This had helped Ian, while James has had no such advantages. But there is another difference between them that is harder to pin down. Gifted children can vary considerably in their personalities. Ian and James seem to have been made out of separate batches of dough, when you meet them. Ian wants to know who you are, and why. James is polite, but less curious; he wants to get back to his friends. You do not *have* to be an extrovert to develop your gifts, but it is certainly a disadvantage to be a shy, reticent, unadventurous child with little confidence in yourself as an independent agent, without the support of friends. Personality helps one, and not the other. Which came first? Success breeds success, and confidence is built up by encouragement. But at birth James inherited some kind of personality mixture, and how far this may have been holding him back is something we can only guess at.

An easy way to account for the Ian-James differences is to point to the fact that Ian has been living with both his parents. Loss of contact with his mother at the age of four must have disturbed James very considerably. It also seems likely that he may have been aware of rows or tension before the split. But he has been lucky in having a secure home, with much love and affection from his great-aunt. Again, his outlook might or might not have been different if his parents had not broken up. Arguably, the tension in his home *might* have been worse, and he might have been less happy.

James is *not* an unhappy child. He is even-tempered, and enjoys a lot of what he does. He certainly has very little—if any—sense of loss where academic work is concerned. That, of course, may come later.

It would be wrong to suppose that a broken home necessarily prejudices a gifted child's chances of doing well. It must affect them, obviously, in many ways. But desire to learn, to master a skill, and to do something at least as well as others appear to do it, can be unaffected. In some cases the child's determination to impress and to attract attention through working hard and well is actually increased; psychologists note that this 'need achievement' can be high when there is something important in the family background—such as the loss of a parent's love—for which a child wants compensation.

In James's case this has not happened. He seems to have been left with a very basic need to belong to a group of children of his own age. He cannot risk doing anything that will threaten his belonging. Possibly he tries hard to do and say things which stamp him more clearly as one of them. At his school, or the group he has fixed on, this includes groaning at most of the teachers' classwork suggestions, and seizing opportunities to look at comics or to play up. Ironically, he is never completely accepted by these others: he is *watching* them too closely, instead of being one of them. Whether he knows he could do some things better if he tried is very much in doubt. This question doesn't really arise for him. His future happiness at school and his preparation for future life may depend on his being coaxed into sensing, and enjoying, achievement. At the same time, he needs self-reliance to go his own way, and this can only grow very gradually.

Not all gifted children 'under-achieve' because they are like James or because they share his difficulties. Sometimes the situation is quite different.

Mary

Mary has needed psychiatric help over the past three years, although now that she is thirteen she has begun to be less dependent on it.

She had always seemed a very bright child. Her parents were very proud of her. She talked early, read early and ran about early. Her mother, a trained teacher, devoted a lot of time to preparing her for school. When she entered the junior section of a select girls' private school at five, she already had a sound idea about how to compose a sentence, and knew that the Stuarts followed the Tudors. She is an only child, which makes this devotion to her early education more understandable. By all accounts she must have been very rewarding to teach, in that she had a stream of logical questions for every new idea or fact that was offered her.

Her first year at her school was a mixture of good and bad. Her teacher was very interested in her, and was very sensitive towards her. But Mary was jolted by the boisterous behaviour of the others, particularly in the cloakroom and the playground. She was also put out, apparently, by the need to take turns, both with equipment and in talking to her teacher. She was a day-girl, while many were boarders and she suspected they were treated as favourites. Thus she was socially backward, and possibly—since her first teacher remembers her as often being reduced to 'a soggy mess'— she was emotionally backward by comparison with the others. She developed a very strong antipathy towards the school after a few weeks; this involved tearful entreaties to be kept at home, tantrums on delivery at the school gate, and bed-wetting on Sunday nights (presumably since Monday morning was looming near). Her parents thought this went on for rather a long time. They talked to the teacher and the headmistress. Then they took her to see an educational psychologist. To put things right the mother decided that the logical thing was to arrange an examination of her daughter: the school might be wrong for Mary's particular talents in an unsuspected way.

The psychologist rapidly concluded that Mary was exceptionally gifted, just as her mother had always believed. Confirmation of this was gratifying, but the judgment that Mary was also 'immature' and 'rather disturbed' was unwelcome. The mother put this down to the fact that her daughter had had a bad cold and was not on top form after a hectic week at school. The psychologist advised against boarding schools and against shifting Mary to the local state primary too. She could not adapt to either, he considered. It was better that she should be encouraged to make friends at her current school, and be helped to concentrate on activities that interested her and did not require a constant interchange with the teacher. It seems that the psychologist felt that there was no more suitable school in the area for treating this kind of child sympathetically. He did, in fact, suggest a Rudolf Steiner school as a possible alternative, but Mary's parents rejected this as not meeting the academic standards they demanded for their child.

For a time Mary seemed to adjust better. Having some girls round to tea and getting used to horseplay with them probably helped.

In the second year Mary had the misfortune to come up against a teacher with very rigid views on teaching. Along with all the others, Mary had to go through the teacher's own syllabus, whether they knew some of it already or not. Mary suffered most because she was further ahead academically, and because her mother visited the school and suggested she should be moved up a class. It seems likely (from talking to other staff) that the teacher took against Mary, even to the point of looking for ways of indicating that 'she's not so clever as everybody makes her out to be'. As a result, Mary resented the tasks she was set that were simply repetition, and developed a blockage against accepting instruction in anything new from her form teacher. She wet her bed, had nightmares and complained about school. The whole problem was reassessed again, but once more it was decided to leave her where she was.

Her work at school became very sketchy. She started things and would not finish them. She complained a lot about having too little time, the wrong book, the wrong pencils, and classmates who interrupted her. Her popularity refused to grow. She had a reputation in the playground for being suddenly very aggressive even if only mildly teased.

While there is no doubt that one teacher was unpleasant if not actually vindictive towards her, most of the teachers who came into contact with her reached the conclusion that she was not nearly as promising or as interesting to teach as had been suggested at first. Only later, when it became obvious that she was very disturbed, did they think in terms of her being very intelligent but held back by emotional problems.

At one time Mary's parents decided that she must be getting lazy. Where were the merit stars at the bottom of her compositions? Where was the evidence that she was developing new skills or talents? She never spoke much about what she did at school, except to complain about teachers, about other girls, about school meals . . . They felt she needed a reminder every now and then that a lot of money was being paid for her education, and that, with the common entrance exam coming along in the not so distant future, she had better pull her proverbial socks up.

When Mary was nine, a lot seemed to happen at once. One day Mary went to a main line railway station instead of getting off with the others at the station near her school. She got past one barrier and was ignored by the guard of her train. About a hundred and fifty miles farther on, she wove an elaborate story to a ticket collector to the effect that she had been separated from her aunt by the crowd; could they please find her. The aunt, a further fifty miles away, was contacted. This lady returned Mary to her parents in due course. Simultaneously, Mary's teacher spoke to her mother about a series of thefts, culminating in the discovery of some of the items in Mary's locker. Then another girl's mother demanded to know why Mary was being allowed to 'torture' her daughter in the playground.

The psychiatrist consulted insisted, to the parents' surprise, on working with the whole family, rather than with Mary, and with the school. This is where he saw the main problem.

Mary represented the chance of getting all those academic distinctions the parents had not quite attained. She was identified—correctly, as it happened—as having the capacity for this. Unfortunately she was groomed for this to the exclusion of much of the ordinary experience of life that helps a child to become mature. It was not the *pushing* by the parents, so much as keeping her away from social contact, from frivolous but amusing and satisfying activities, that had left Mary incapable of dealing with the situation at school. They had also given her the impression that their love and respect for her were very closely bound up with her academic success. When she failed, or was below their standard, this put her in an intolerable position of which they were barely, if at all, conscious. When things went wrong at school they were inclined to think in terms of bad teaching, or of Mary pausing before accelerating. It took the emergence of some very clear-cut behaviour problems before they reappraised their own standpoint. And even then they criticized the psychiatrist for spending so much time talking to *them*, when he should have concentrated entirely on their daughter.

Two things have been in Mary's favour since the crisis point. The first is that her parents have come round to accepting the fact that Mary may eventually shine in some activity that has very little to do with formal academic distinction. They are in effect putting her mental health first. Secondly, although Mary would have been sent home from many a school, a very responsible line was taken by her headmistress: it was realized that, if Mary was to be helped, expulsion—however tactfully explained—was bad policy. The school felt some responsibility in the matter themselves.

There is a simple contrast to be drawn between James and Mary. James had parents (and a guardian) whose expectations for his education were too low, while Mary's parents probably set an impossible standard. But this is a bit over-simple. Parents have every right to differ about the importance of passing exams and getting impressive pieces of paper. It is when education occupies a disproportionate place in their priorities that serious problems arise. If they deprecate 'all this book learning' on the one hand, or demand from their child regular details of the day's latest scholastic triumphs on the other, they have a strange sense of proportion. Some gifted children seem, in fact, to have the strength of mind to rise above each of these viewpoints: they survive, and sometimes write books about their home life. These may tend to exaggerate the power of the child to transcend his upbringing, especially since little is read of the children who do not write such books.

Mary might have met her parents' expectations, but circumstances were against it. It is impossible to disentangle the effect of the form teacher who took against her from the other influence. But the effect is not all that uncommon with gifted children. A hard-working teacher has to aim at the average. If he (or she) is attracted by the personality of some child who is backward or gifted, there will be an incentive to devote some special time to his particular needs too. An unattractive personality may produce the opposite effect. Teachers may express their feelings by saying that a gifted child 'is getting above himself', that he 'needs to learn how to do things thoroughly' (as an excuse for getting him to follow the form's pace rather than build on what he knows); and maybe that he 'must learn that he's not the only pebble on the beach', to discourage him from asking too many questions. (These are *actual* comments, made recently.)

A gifted child can represent a threat to a teacher. He has a knack of asking difficult questions; of seeming to have his *own* sources of information, thus by-passing the teacher; of wanting to extend class projects into areas not yet fully explored; and he may seem set for a better career, academic or otherwise, than the teacher's own. Resentment can set in, and the child is at risk.

Most people have to survive at least one bad experience with an unsympathetic teacher. Cheerful survival is perfectly possible. But a really determined teacher can seriously constrict the desire for learning and the excitement of stretching one's mind, in a gifted child. Being intelligent, the child may adapt sensibly to a new situation: if it makes for a quieter life, with fewer sardonic comments, it makes sense not to try to stand out but to keep one's light firmly under a bushel. This in turn may convince many that the child never was as bright as all that anyway. In reality, an under-achieving gifted child may be two steps ahead. But under-achievement may become a habit.

Here is a comment by the headmaster of a state primary school on *Alexandra*, who is highly gifted and very inquisitive:

I feel you should really be thinking about a different school for her. She undoubtedly needs more expert teaching and probably more individual contact with a really good teacher than I can provide. My teachers *are* very good . . . but they are not graduates. The kind of questions that Alex keeps asking sends them scurrying to the encyclopaedia in my study. The other day I saw two of the staff spending half their lunch hour working out how the atom was split so they could explain it to her. She's a wonderful child, but this is not the right place.

This headmaster was right about his staff. They tried to adapt. Not every primary teacher would. They had worked hard too at minimizing the sense of otherness which could easily have grown up between her and the other children. They got her to take roles in drama sessions that were slapstick, and gave 'leader' roles to others. They tried to praise all their children according to effort, rather than achievement. But Alexandra proved too much for them in the end.

Alexandra is pretty, well-spoken, nice-mannered and eager without being 'pushy'. Had she been an overweight boy with spots and spectacles, who sniffed, demanded 'What?' querulously and whined, even these very helpful teachers might have tried cutting him down to size. Improving his manners might have been desirable, but cutting off stimulation and setting him against the school system would not.

Some experts have estimated that about 85 per cent of gifted children, while young, are not only emotionally stable but enjoy better adjustment at home and at school than the average. The other 15 per cent are sometimes ill favoured, although this is not always the case. Being less superficially lovable, they may be less popular with staff as well as other children. If their manners are bad, too, the disadvantage is more than doubled. The ones who need most help are probably the ones who seem the least approachable.

Seven
Early effects on the family

A gifted child is not without problems. He may be misunderstood, resented, and his natural talents may be ignored or stifled. But whatever happens to him and to his gifts, he can have a profound effect on his family too. This chapter considers the problems that his parents and his brothers and sisters can experience, and what can be done about them.

A good deal depends on how far the parents are prepared for the advent of a gifted child. Are they confident? Agreeably surprised? Or totally uninterested? Or thoroughly alarmed? Any combination of these reactions is possible, bearing in mind that a mother and a father do not always have similar backgrounds or the same educational interests.

When two parents have a good educational background, a record of academic success and a strong sense of cultural values, they are generally pleased to see signs of high intelligence in their child. Possibly they half expect it—which may cause problems if their child has not got high intelligence. But they encourage the first words he uses, and show him all kinds of different things to feel and see and play with. All this must help. They have expectations, however, which may put them on a collision course that will not help anyone.

They may have set ideas about the ways in which high intelligence should be directed. If the child is a genuine all-rounder, this may not produce a crisis. If, however, he has particular inclinations, which meet the approval and encouragement of his teachers but not of his parents, or of one parent but not the other, there is an obvious chance of friction. It is very easy to say, in a detached way, 'I am a senior civil servant, who has depended on good exam results and clear, logical exposition of facts and arguments to get where I am. But where my son is concerned, I am content that he should make the most of whatever talents he has, even if they are completely different from mine.' It is quite another thing to *mean* it. For such a man, the concept that education actually *equals* academic qualifications may be very hard to set aside. His gifted son or daughter may show little promise of getting to what he feels is 'a good school' on merit. Instead, there may be a lot of exhibits brought home that may not seem particularly artistic even, by the standards to which he is used. Absence of progress in arithmetic and languages may seem like 'a waste', which depresses him over time. Meanwhile, the child's talents may be unfolding, very slowly, in the direction of something like stained glass or scenery design, or an art for which words are used in ways that have not been imagined yet. Mother may approve while father fumes—or rather, cannot understand that this might be a satisfying career whether there is money at the end of it or not.

Similarly, the parents may reach a crisis if a gifted child shows particular skills that are usually associated with the opposite sex. This may be more likely as a problem with a gifted child simply because the attainments in the chosen area become strikingly obvious, more quickly. A later chapter will deal with role definitions in a broader sense. Here the point is worth making that discord in the family can be generated by the problem of how to react to a boy who is precocious at making clothes for dolls, or to a girl who likes tinkering with engines and shows she is good at it.

There is no doubt that some schools may be excellent

places for learning particular subjects or skills, but will undoubtedly reduce the chances of a child making progress in interests that do not fit neatly into the curriculum. Some would go further and claim that the store that these schools set by scholarships and so forth actively stifles those interests, so that it is only the conscious rebel who maintains them. The parents of a gifted child who does not easily conform may find that the question of choice of school is a very serious challenge to marital harmony. Of course this can affect any household. But consciousness that a child has special gifts can accentuate the feeling of responsibility, and give rise to anxiety that bad placement might spoil everything that seemed so promising.

Sometimes, too, parents with a broad background of culture and education may be taken by surprise by a gifted child's speed and persistence of inquiry. They may not have been gifted themselves. They may remember school, or they may have seen other children regarding school, as a long, hard grind. What does it mean, then, when this child of theirs pesters them, at four, with questions about their car and how it works? Why doesn't he need to sleep at the proper time? Why doesn't he go off and play with the others, instead of hanging round and trying to join in adult conversations? Here again parents may be entirely agreed on how to treat this. They may decide that this behaviour borders on impertinence and should be discouraged. Then one may feel that perhaps he should be treated differently from their conventional view of what is right and what is not. A gifted child may seem to threaten a neat pattern whereby a hard-working father and mother can study their Sunday papers at leisure at the weekend, with the toddlers safely in a sandpit. When the toddlers want to know what's going on in those papers and are desperate to learn to read some, there is often trouble.

But this may be minimal compared with the disruption that a gifted child can cause in a home where there is no, or very little, cultural or educational tradition. Here the need to relax in spare time may be felt more strongly, and the difference between thinking up a good answer for a tricky question and relaxation as they understand it may be all the greater. The fact that gifted children often seem to need less sleep is a serious matter to them. Keeping one of them quiet with pop music or television may work for a while, but his tolerance of a situation in which he is expected to be a passive listener or watcher may be much shorter than his parents'. He will want to ask questions about what he sees and hears, and when he is bored—which may be soon—he will look for a new stimulus. In many ways he will not correspond to what his parents have experienced, or understand from friends' and relatives' experience, as natural activity for a young child, even when still an infant. Therefore he may be looked on as odd or naughty, and (on either count) he will inspire them to try to correct him. Because this will be only partly successful and will probably lead to *real* behaviour problems, the parents are likely to be depressed and possibly divided about what is happening. Gradually one of the parents may perceive their child as a threat because his interests, his curiosity, and his questions are constant reminders of past academic failure, and the present need is to look up and find out some answers.

It may seem far-fetched to claim that serious marital problems can arise from difficulties over a gifted child. It is well known that handicapped children can, tragically, impose severe strains to the point of divorce. (This happens not all that rarely—not so much because of the child or what he does as because of the inadequacy of social services to help, the attitudes of friends and relations, and the restrictions that looking after the child involves.) But a gifted child is handicapped too. If he becomes frustrated and disturbed, or if one parent decides that he (or she) alone understands him, the results can be dire for the marriage.

These are situations where early preparation for having a gifted child is important. One of the most significant steps in recent years has been the growth of concern over gifted children shown by the Department of Health and Social Security. There have been courses run for health officers by the National Association for Gifted Children. The DHSS has considered it important enough to build an awareness of how possible gifted children may be recognized into the training organized for health visitors and those who are to staff child guidance clinics.

This means that, in addition to looking for early signs of mental handicap, health visitors will be on the look-out for indications that a child may be showing promise of being gifted. Obviously, they may be *wrong*. It would be intolerable for well-meaning health visitors to go round encouraging parents to expect the most from children who will inevitably disappoint them later. But if they are carefully trained to open the door, very gently, to the possibility of special intelligence, then parents will have a much better idea of what may be coming to them.

If parents are told that their bewilderingly active little baby is at least a recognizable type—far from being freakish—then this must in itself be reassuring to them. As it becomes clearer that the early signs (e.g. raising the head and following objects with the eyes) are succeeded by excellent co-ordination and early speech, together with a minimal sleep need, a compulsion to explore, and the ability to concentrate on something engrossing for long periods, then the possibility of very high intelligence may be mooted. Coming like this it may be less of a shock. (Contrary to much 'intellectual' opinion, many parents do not want a very intelligent child: clever, yes, and inheriting special skills, yes, but 'intelligence' and the undesirable comparisons and the bookishness which that implies— decidedly no.) But gradually being shown the kinds of activities which it can be particularly rewarding to introduce to a gifted child can certainly soften the blow. To be effective, this recognition and discussion of a child's possible talents should start when the child is young.

Those parents who have fixed ideas about the paths their gifted child should tread do not want advice on helping them. They can always argue that what was good for them cannot be all that bad for their children. There will be a measure of truth in this: it is at least arguable. But they may be misjudging the times as well as their child's temperament, personality and talents.

In the future, it has been argued, it may be particularly important to encourage two kinds of giftedness. One is originality in thinking: in particular, maintaining an objective view about the desirability of a system while learning all about it, and how its functions might be optimized. The second is the kind of genius that transcends individual brilliance: teamwork in which each highly intelligent member is contributing towards a result that no individual could contrive. The argument for the increased importance of both these manifestations of giftedness lies in the concept of accelerating change. The pace at which business needs, business pressures, and social and political considera-tions are all changing is, in most respects, getting faster all the time. Innovations need a group to conceive, plan and execute them—whether they are in a laboratory, a factory or a marketing team. Apart from the value to society of helping its brain power to apply itself in ways that are relevant to the age, the individual gifted person is more likely to feel that he is fulfilling himself if he senses that he is going to be taking part in the changing, as opposed to being changed.

It is not necessary to go along with these arguments in their entirety in order to conclude that certain routes such as Dragon–Eton–Oxbridge–Harvard Business School–Shell should not be regarded as automatically suitable for a clever child however admirable and beneficial they may have seemed up to this point. If the events and atmosphere along that career route are shown to be adapting themselves to the educational and social needs of the time, and to the individual person's talent and character, then that raises other issues which must influence judgment. It is the assumptions underlying questions like 'Isn't it time he was learning Latin?' or 'When on earth is he going to meet up with the Second Law of Thermodynamics?' that need to be questioned.

This applies to girls too. The nature of role definition for women is changing, faster than many mothers care to admit. Whereas, in the past pressure from society tended to direct women towards social work and coffee mornings once the more continuous demands of looking after their children had lapsed, it is now the woman who does *not* go back to a career when the children are at school who is often forced to be defensive. In broad social changes of this kind, people often tend to lose sight of the individual, and what is right for her. Again, the automatic assumption that long training in science may be wasteful or unsuitable for a girl in comparison with, say, a teacher's training course envisaged as an 'insurance policy' in case of failure to marry or failure of a marriage, is the kind of attitude that needs re-examination. If it means that a gifted girl is discouraged from pursuing a subject that fascinates

her and arouses her talent, it will frustrate her and introduce a bone of contention between parents that can be long-
lasting.

These children do not present problems for their parents
alone. The brothers and sisters of a gifted child may be
entirely without the special intelligence that marks him out
from them. Life can be made specially hard, if the gifted
child is preferred to them. He may get all the attention, and
more affection. He may be an object of wonder and
enthusiasm. He is the one that neighbours and relatives ask
about, eager for news of the latest triumphs. What can they
do in these circumstances?

It is often the case that educational and child guidance
counselling are needed more by the brother and sister of a
gifted child than by the young genius himself. If the parents
have blinded themselves to the effects of imbalance in the
interest they show for each child, they can be very surprised
when a psychologist looks round the family and points this
out to them.

Georgie and Frances

Georgie's first day at her primary school began with a
teacher looking her up and down and saying, 'So you're
Frances's sister! Well, we should be sure of one bright spark
in the class, then.'

Gradually, Georgie became less and less comfortable, as
the real state of affairs came to light. When Frances had
started primary school she could read fluently, she had a
good understanding of money as a basis for doing sums,
and she could draw rather well. Georgie could read her own
name, she could distinguish silver coins from copper, and
she drew circles with huge fingers attached if asked to 'do a

picture of Mummy'. She felt the other children were all doing 'rather hard things'. Although she cannot remember any actual words used, she has a clear impression of the teacher's face growing longer with disappointment. Frances had shone at everything and had just taken her place in the local grammar school, with a special prize for her performance in the 11-plus exam. How Georgie was to maintain the tradition was not at all clear.

There seems little doubt that Frances was a gifted child; she had an IQ assessment only when an adult, but the result clearly points that way. She is a doctor now, specializing in a little-known branch of medicine after taking a first class honours degree at university. Shortly, she will be submitting her thesis for a D.Phil.

Georgie feels that both she and her brother have always been in Frances's shadow. When Georgie was given a grammar school place she was told it was not because of her exam marks, but because her sister was at the school. She remembers moments of agony when she could not understand her homework, and Frances was deputed by her parents to help her out. 'But I explained all this to you last week!' Frances would say. Simply hearing this used to make Georgie feel numb and made it impossible for her to grasp the explanation when it was repeated.

Georgie's parents seem to have alternated between thinking that she was less industrious than her sister, or less intelligent. In fact, both theories were right. Georgie did not enjoy struggling at what Frances had sailed through with ease. Anything that involved a comparison, Georgie avoided if at all possible, with the result that she was slow even by her own standards to master a lot of school subjects. She was accused of being lazy and resented the subjects even more. She discovered several enjoyable ways of rebelling against the school system, including truancy and forming a gang.

Her mother perceived that Georgie was very jealous, and apparently inferior at most things. Frances's gifts did not extend to tact until she was older, which caused friction in the household. The mother decided, very wisely, that Georgie needed some activity or skill that she could develop alone. She was given riding lessons to which—to Frances's disgust—she went by herself. This was to be 'Georgie's thing'.

Without realizing it, Georgie had contrived a similar situation at school. Her sister had excelled at tennis, so she took up swimming. Both riding and swimming Georgie found she could be good at, and good enough, in time, to become an instructor in each. A side-effect was that sport consumed so much of her time and attention that her academic work suffered even more. Yet, when she found a branch of English literature on the syllabus that Frances had missed, she managed to get an 'A' level in this subject.

Ben, her younger brother, went to a secondary modern school. Even there, he too was aware of having his progress measured against that of Frances. His place of refuge was in motorcycle engines, which he learned about by talking with older boys at a nearby garage. He was soon able to strip them down, and emphasized his maleness by coming into meals with black hands, and by becoming the despair of his teachers. Ben has never passed any exams, except for one in engineering. This has helped him, and so has his determination to prove his parents' fears are groundless by making a successful career in scrap metal and second-hand cars. He is making money; at the same time he is so negative towards education and everything that goes with it that he will only tolerate the briefest of interviews about it.

Georgie and Ben admit that there have been times in their childhood when they would cheerfully have torn Frances limb from limb. Even now there is little contact between her and them. Their parents regret that there was so much competitive spirit in the household. But they see this as being partly due to the education system and partly an expression of each of their children's personality. 'I wish they wouldn't always be trying to settle old scores,' their mother says.

I have chosen an analysis of this family to illustrate brothers' and sisters' problems because it is a mixture of light and dark. Georgie and Ben never went before a magistrate, and have had no need of sedatives or prolonged psychiatric help. Nevertheless, they were put at a considerable disadvantage.

Brothers and sisters are going to be envious of each other to some extent, whatever happens. One is bound to seem luckier than another. Parents are not perfect, and they cannot scrupulously dole out equal portions of love in strict rotation. What is less common, and bad for everyone, is a long progression of events, each tending to make one member of a family inferior to another.

In an ideal world, both mental handicap and giftedness would be accepted as items which can affect any child in any family, and be regarded as similar to having red hair, or being tall and strong. Children need to be able to feel pride in making the most of what they have: each one in the family should feel that he or she can and will do just that.

The problem is that children are often competitive, with no prompting from parents whatever. Biologically it makes sense that brothers and sisters should have developed this way, so that each is making sure that one is not getting less food or protection than another. It seems like an instinct for survival. Some would say it is an inevitable by-product of 'attachment behaviour'—the instinctive need to share earliest experiences with one's mother and to remain as close to her as possible—when two children are pressing their claims at once. This theory would suggest that the best foundation for self-confidence in the family (so that competitiveness can be kept within reasonable bounds) must be a very close, warm relationship between mother and each infant in its earliest years—say, up to the age of five.

This is the period within which any tendency to lavish more concern over a different child, who is older or within the same age bracket, must have its most dispiriting effect. This is the time at which a child will identify a basic threat to his attachment, and will form a clear and lasting association between danger and the young paragon whose tricks are being admired so much.

When all the children in a family are made to feel that each has got a rich mixture of understanding and love, one child may still envy another's talent, but without the intensity that is reserved for a threat to his position.

Apart from this general prescription, there are several other positive steps that parents can take to help non-gifted children.

1. The first is not to assume that because one child is gifted, the others must be too. The others may be entirely average in intelligence. Let evidence of further giftedness in the family come from the child: it cannot be coaxed or forced out of him.
2. Your gifted child may have beautiful models and drawings and neat exercise books to bring back from nursery or primary school. These are *achievements*. His twin sister may have some nondescript objects which she brings home with her. They represent *effort*—possibly more than went into producing the achievements. As such, and as gifts to her parents, they are very important to her. She must be talked to and

encouraged about these as well as her brother. Otherwise, it is a short step to believing that 'he can do it, and he can please Mummy. But I can't'.

3. A gifted child is usually more articulate, and can phrase criticism more accurately and sharply. Sometimes he will be merciless. Show that you feel he has better things to do than pouring scorn on a brother's or sister's efforts.

4. Shared activities help put a damper on competitiveness, when it is threatening to turn the home into a bullring. Music, tree-houses, making large models indoors, listening to stories, talking about ideas, holidays, projects—all these can be, but are not necessarily, shared. Very young children usually play independently and they start making something together, but end up apart. This should not stop parents from organizing and encouraging a sense of doing things together, not as weapons to be used against each other.

5. Part of the day should belong to each child: during this time others may be told, gently but firmly, to keep to one side. Children may seem to resent, but are generally great supporters of, the principle of 'turns'. Everyone knows that—whatever the other has or has not achieved—each will get a turn in the end.

6. Sometimes a gifted child will propel a family conversation beyond the limits of the other children even (sometimes) when they are older than he is. Parents need to be expert judges of wavelength if they are to stop the other children feeling left out of it, while not denying the gifted child opportunities for adult-to-adult discussion. Changing the level of conversation, as in this example from a family where the elder child (age nine) is gifted, and his sister (age six) is very intelligent, but not gifted, is a useful knack to develop:

Alan: 'What have you brought back from the party, Freda?'

Freda: 'It's a magic painting book.'

Mother: 'Shall I show you how the magic works, Freda?'

Alan: 'It's not really magic, you know.'

Freda: 'Yes it is!'

Alan: 'No it's not. It's done with anhydrous paints. Part of the picture, that policeman's uniform, will have copper sulphate stuck to the paper in tiny, tiny bits of crystal. When you put some water on it the bits turn from white to blue. Let me show—'

Mother: 'Do you know what the other chemicals are likely to be, for the other colours?'

Alan: 'I'm not sure.'

Mother: 'You go and look them up, then, in your chemistry book. I'll be interested to know. Freda, you can bring me a glass of water and a paint brush, and we'll see how to make the magic colours come up.'

7. Georgie's mother made her daughter a much happier and more satisfied girl when she arranged for her to go riding, leaving the tennis court to her sister. This was an intelligent move. When a gifted child is a brilliant all-rounder, good at sport as well as every school subject, finding a suitable niche for a brother or sister to flourish and take pride in can be very difficult. Riding is a solution that will be too expensive or inconvenient for many people. But there are many other possibilities. Making a collection, singing in a choir, playing a musical instrument, joining the Scouts or Guides, sailing, rowing, judo, pottery or going to help on a farm—all these are possible,

depending on where you live. But it requires sensitivity and tact in judging whether a child and an activity will become good friends. Then, encouragement will be needed to show him you regard it as important, and not just a soft option for the less intelligent. Encouragement must stop if it is obvious that the child's curiosity is satisfied and that he derives no pleasure from it. You may need to try several openings before the right one appears.

8. A less intelligent child's friends may seem less desirable as companions than those cultivated by a gifted child. But showing disapproval of such friends is the highroad towards losing communication. If a gifted child's brother or sister is popular among a group, compliment their popularity. It means a lot to them.

9. Think very carefully about sending two children of very different abilities to the same school. Even if you try not to make comparisons in how they get on, you can be certain that some teacher will. This has to be balanced against how well the two get on, and whether they seem to need the occasional sight of each other during the day. Certain types of school do not go in for marking exercises or publishing 'league tables' showing how high or low each child is placed—at least up to the age of ten. These are better places for mixed ability children. Montessori schools are a good example. These have an atmosphere where practically everyone can feel a winner, since the equipment and methods used allow for each child within an age group to proceed at his own pace, and feel happy through being stretched to attain what is within his particular grasp.

There is an obvious problem where the gifted child gets a

scholarship to, say, Eton, and there are neither funds nor a place to be won for his sister anywhere than at the local comprehensive school. This may prove to be a very good school for her, but she may well grow up to resent the way her education was 'sacrificed' to pay for her brother's tail-coats. Much depends on her personality, on what she enjoys and what she achieves, but bitterness and strong inverted snobbery are not unknown in these circumstances. 'Sibling rivalry' is something that is largely inevitable. It is exacerbated when the odds against one rival having many wins to his credit are high. This is when parents may have to be alert, and defuse situations before they can explode. They should realize that they can never succeed *entirely* in this. But the effort is worth while if it makes the family happier.

Eight
What can parents do?

Anything suggested in this chapter must take second place to one basic consideration. This is that any child, gifted or not, will grow up into a happier individual if he is both loved and respected by both his parents. Some children are simply not *liked* by their parents. It happens. Nothing I write will materially affect this point. 'Respect' may seem an odd word to those who hold that their children's first duty is to respect *them*. But in a relationship that is both happy and positive, respect has to work both ways. A child's individuality—the fact that he is a distinct personality, with his own interests and talents and later, probably, with his own values—has to be respected if he is going to be spontaneously warm and considerate, as opposed to feeling bound by guilt, or having to struggle to be separate. This point seems particularly important where gifted children are concerned: all the evidence shows that they develop and want to express individual opinions early on. Many are very precocious in their demand to talk, be heard and discuss at an adult level. Sometimes they will make mistakes, and sometimes they will be gauche or rude: there is no point in letting all this go by, but it must be equally wrong to resent precocious-ness and curiosity if these are part of their nature simply because they are not 'suitable' for children.

The easiest way to begin is to suggest what parents should *avoid*: first, over-reaction to the news that your child is gifted; parents on learning this must, quite obviously, feel rather differently about their child especially if it comes as a big surprise. It should be a rather exciting discovery, although it is certainly alarming to some. But this is no reason for changing your whole approach to him.

Dale's mother recalls:

When our daughter was found to have a very high IQ, my husband couldn't believe it at first. It seemed extraordinary to him that she should have more brain power than either of our two sons, although it didn't exactly surprise me . . . Every now and then he seemed to want to test her out, just to see if it was true. This was when she was six, and literally one day he was swinging her up in the air and calling her chatterbox, and the next he was tip-toeing up to her and saying 'Dale, what happens if you take 3 away from 21?' Sometimes he'd satisfy himself that the test was all wrong, and sometimes he'd not be sure, and he'd just watch her from the corner of the room. I don't know what Dale made of it, I'm sure—but it unnerved me. In the end we had to agree not to talk about it in front of her, and not to ask her a lot of questions. We agreed we should read with her, and talk about things she used to ask us (which we'd usually laughed at before), but try to be natural with her, just as with her two brothers.

This illustrates very well what sometimes happens. If it goes on, the situation can be reached when the parents treat their gifted child in an entirely different way from other children and from others in the family. This has several unfortunate consequences if the difference is sharp. He is likely to get an exaggerated opinion of himself which will increase difficulties at the school, and will expose him to a considerable shock when he *does* meet his intellectual equals. He will be unpopular with other children, too, which may be worse for him in the long term. In a family of two brothers, if one senses that the other is getting special attention, possibly bordering on the deferential, by evidence of some skill or talent that isn't fully discussed in the open, the chance of resentment is very high indeed. If both brothers are naughty together, both should be remonstrated with in similar terms: otherwise a division is being created between them.

'I don't know how my parents stood for James,' says Karen, who is above average in intelligence but not gifted. James has an IQ of 160 and a very considerable gift for mathematics. Karen continued:

When he was at his primary school, everyone got very excited about what he could do with numbers. You know, he could do square roots and cube roots in his head, and he used to make mathematical figures and label them. He was a terrible show-off. Whenever anybody came to dinner, I would be up because I'm four years older, but he'd come down in his pyjamas, shout hello, run around, refuse to go back to bed, interrupt people when they were talking, and ask the guests what day they were born, so that he could tell them which day of the week it had been. Once or twice he'd seize a glass of sherry or something, out of a guest's hand, and swig it. Mummy used to say 'Oh dear!' and 'Please, James,' but it never did any good. Daddy just used to pretend he wasn't there. They apologized for him, once he finally went to bed, and that gave them the excuse for talking about how well he was doing and how difficult it was finding him the right school. Of course James has got a remarkable brain, and once he started at boarding school things got much better. But I don't understand why anyone ever came back to have dinner with us a second time.

This illustrates the need for another 'don't'. As well as avoiding a situation where a child is encouraged to believe he is Einstein reincarnate, and that as such he is above the ordinary requirements of polite or social behaviour, there is the point of not becoming a Gifted Child Bore.

If the visitors to your home and their children seem to hear you talk about nothing except your gifted child's triumphs, problems and expectations, you are ensuring his unpopularity. This applies however pleasant and modest he may actually be. Giving him a reputation as a conversation-stopper is like shooting an albatross and hanging it round his neck.

Of course one cannot not talk about one's own child, especially if he is doing something interesting. But the rule ought to be, that for every comment about your gifted child you must make at least one about another child in your family and/or ask a question about your friend's children. Or discuss local politics.

Connected with this problem is the danger of giving your child the impression that it is because he is gifted that you find him especially interesting. He should be clear in his mind that his importance to you is *as your child*, and for no other reason. Otherwise, he becomes emotionally dependent on success, to an extent which cannot be justified; he cannot always hope to maintain this, given that he has little or no control when young over the subjects he is taught, the way he is taught them, or the nature of the teachers. When the point is reached that missing top marks is accompanied by a sinking feeling that 'Mum and Dad are not going to like this', a child faces each day as if it were a major examination. His energy is directed towards mastery of a subject, not understanding or appreciation; this mastery involves demonstration of skill in a competitive spirit, which has very little to do with getting to know what a subject has to offer and enjoying learning about it. Apart from the risk of emotional crisis, fostering this feeling in a child is in many cases an incentive to him to stage a full-scale revolt against the educational system when he is older and against many other systems too—any, in fact, which he can group under 'establishment' or 'bourgeois values'.

Adam, now twenty-two, recalls that as a young child he was singled out in class at seven as 'good scholarship material'. His parents were very pleased with him. Every Sunday afternoon his father used to sit with him and go over all the schoolwork he had been doing during the week. They would then discuss things like electricity, or how the solar system works, and his father would give him a little test after tea on the ground they had covered. When his father returned home from work in the evening he used always to query whether homework had been done, especially if he saw Adam playing with a train.

He remembers his mother in those days for her great anxiety to know how the others in his class were doing. Why had Christopher got more gold stars than he had? 'Because Miss Bennett says he tries very hard although he doesn't always get things right.' 'Don't *you* try very hard, Adam?'

He was, in fact, scholarship material. He passed everything he tried for, despite (as he recalls) wishing and praying that the next test might be the last. When he had taken his 'A' levels at his public school, he went through a basic change of outlook:

I realize now that I'd been *used*. My parents set fire to me just so that they could feel warm inside. I can't remember when, exactly, or how it was I suddenly understood—but I think it was talking to some friends at school about what they were going to do later, and what their parents expected from them. I knew, then, that we'd all been conned.

Adam announced one day that he was 'pulling out'. He has not gone to university, as had been planned, and he has carefully avoided anything that seemed like a conventional job with a career structure. He lives in a house with eight other like-minded militant politicians. He organizes squatters into untenanted property, joins in demonstrations if the cause seems right, and has a suspended sentence for 'disturbing the peace'. Occasionally he makes a little money by writing for a magazine or picking fruit. He reckons that supermarkets are fair game for anyone who is hungry.

Who is to say that Adam is *wrong*? He dislikes what he calls the rat-race and has escaped. But whether his activities against established order are laudable or not, he is very bitter about his parents, his upbringing and his schools. He rejects any activity which seems to have any connection with the academic work (mainly languages and history) that he used to do. He takes pleasure in anything where intellectual thought seems suspended or insulted—such as smoking pot, reading children's comics, or physical confrontations with authority. He makes strong assertions that he is much happier now: they seem too strong to be entirely true, although he is undeniably 'free'.

What is certain—and his parents are prepared to admit as much—is that Adam was not a very happy child. Whether Adam's service to society has been lost is arguable, but loss of happiness is real.

However intelligent a child is, it is very rarely that he stops being a child, in respect of his emotions at least. In fact intellectual acceleration sometimes seems to be bought

at the price of slowing down the pace of social development. When a child has his energies mainly directed
towards things, as opposed to people, there is no gain in knowledge about how people react to each other and how they
judge when it is right to give and take, when to express and
when to conceal disappointment. Education ought to be on
a broader front. But there is no substitute for playing with
other children: no event organized by adults can provide a
similar chance of learning to grow up socially and emotionally. If parents suspect that skylarking around a garden is
a waste of a gifted child's time, it is worth their while to
observe children's games more closely.

Many fantasy games that children play involve two
complementary elements—'working through' and 'rehearsal'. When a child is alarmed by something (whether it
be an angry adult or a scene on television), there is a period
during which he says nothing or very little about it. Later,
he feels a compulsion to talk about it which can be irritating
or embarrassing to others but always salutary to the child.
Adults go through the same 'working through' phase, after
silence following a serious shock, as many psychologists
(from Freud to Sargant) have noted. Fantasy games allow
reconstruction of alarming situations in circumstances over
which the child has or shares control with other children.
They can 'work through' common problems this way, and
by learning from each other they can anticipate or 'rehearse'
others.

Even when a fantasy element is lacking, children can give
each other a better basis for emotional development in
their play. Esther and Tricia were born within a month of each
other. Esther showed she was gifted musically by the time
she was five. Tricia has a very high IQ (at the gifted level)
but has taken much longer to become an 'achiever' at
school. Whenever the two girls played with each other,

between the ages of five to seven, they worked out very elaborate systems whereby they could remain on good terms. They apply these systems relatively rarely when playing with others. A typical example is a series of races they organized across Esther's garden, when aged five. Sometimes they had to go round the edge, sometimes across the middle, sometimes over orange boxes erected as 'jumps'. But each time it was arranged that first Esther would win, then Tricia, then Esther, etc. Turns were strictly observed—despite the fact that Tricia was the stronger runner. They worked out similar rituals for not offending each other at hide-and-seek, French cricket, and even racing model cars. Interestingly, their mothers were, and are, competitive, and compare their children's achievements. By contrast Esther and Tricia are fiercely competitive with other children, but never with each other. They learnt very quickly that this was the wrong approach to each other. Later, they developed elaborate rituals for use whenever either of them did something clever or was praised by her mother in the other's presence. This involved a declaration that it would be 'wonderful to be as clever as you, Esther/Tricia', which had to be answered with 'But I can't . . . like you can, Tricia/Esther.' They don't need to do this any longer. But at the time it prevented them from losing each other's friendship despite their mothers' determination to compare them. It also gave them a social repertoire to use with others, when their popularity was threatened. Had their play been over-organized, or had they not been allowed free time to let off steam with each other, this would not have happened.

André presented, at twelve, a very good example of a child who had, largely because of his very considerable musical gift, had a lot of childhood denied to him. By this age, he was a pianist of talent who had been withdrawn from school so that he could practise seven hours a day, supplemented with two lessons a week. He was entirely serious in his approach to music and his mother encouraged serious pursuits and conversation in the evenings to supplement his lack of formal study in literature and the other arts. (This was easier to arrange in France than in this country.)

When André was brought to England to visit John, a boy of the same age who was also a gifted young pianist, his mother was worried (although the trip would 'be a holiday for him' and broaden his experience of travel prior to making foreign tours) that the three-and-a-half hours of practice that John put in were so inadequate as to create a bad example.

John recalls that André was pleasant, but rather brittle in personality. He could not be teased, or even mildly criticized, without an emotional problem appearing. 'What surprised him most,' John adds, 'was the way I would come to the piano when he'd had an hour or so's exercises, and I'd say "That's enough of that—now let's try this Walton arrangement, it's great fun!" The idea that anything could be "fun" at the piano was totally beyond him.' André, apparently, enjoyed his stay. But it must have been an odd experience, to be in an atmosphere where you could let your hair down occasionally—even in the comparatively mild way described above.

By all accounts, André is still socially immature.

One of the big questions for parents of a young gifted child is how far to stretch or adapt the family routine for his benefit. If he is the first and only child there may be very little problem. But even so, he may not seem childlike enough for a routine ever to be established. He may need little sleep; he may need much more stimulation than a small garden or a television set can provide; he may demonstrate his curiosity by exploring the workings of various machines, the innards of his father's briefcase, or the mysteries of his mother's cosmetics case: *on consecutive days.*

There is no better advice than to be prepared to compromise. No child can be made to sleep more—although the Victorians used laudanum and even gas taps for this purpose. But he can be told to play quietly. If he is desperately bored, he can be shown something interesting— like the way a typewriter works, or how to draw a spaceship. But he can be told firmly 'Mummy is going to put her feet up now and read the paper.' Then, *give* him things to explore before he takes them. The other children may need their toys protected from his depredations, not because he is mean, but because he has more inspiration about how they might be used. Somehow he needs to be persuaded not to seize or abuse what isn't his, without stemming his urge to discover and to improvise.

Many gifted children have a very good sense of occupying themselves once they have got an idea and the right material. If the idea is strong enough, they will find material to use whether it is right or not, and concentrate on the task they have set themselves so singlemindedly as to be 'easy children'. It follows that parents can make life easier for themselves if they watch the *pace* of their children and judge the right time to discuss or suggest ideas, to talk about material that may or may not be used, and supervise, encourage and so forth until it's obvious that they will be happily occupied for some time to come. Put like this, it just sounds like commonsense. But adapting your timing to their timing is often very difficult. Two mothers of gifted children told me that this aspect of handling bright four-year-olds 'makes me feel like a benevolent prison warder'.

However easy they become, they will be thoroughly badly behaved, on occasion—just like any children. Telling them off or criticizing is only natural. You will *not* stunt a genius's growth this way.

Sometimes frustration at not having everything perfect for the activity they want to pursue has this meaning: they don't really *want* to get on with that idea you suggested and which they are making such a fuss over getting started—they really want to help *you*. Boy *or* girl, they might want to sit in the kitchen and watch you make pastry, or help you thin out seedlings in the garden, or pass tools along a work-bench, or put curtain hooks into Rufflette tape. They prefer involvement to watching, of course, and if they know you discourage this they take out their feelings on the 'children's' activities you try to divert them into. Giving them a small part to play or a means of copying your work can help a lot. A young gifted child can make jam tarts from a wedge of the pastry you are using, or can call out percentages off a slide rule to help somebody with statistics to work out. Or he can be given a gimlet, two blocks of wood, a screw and a screwdriver. A gifted child will often rate this kind of thing more highly than a toy, particularly if using it means copying an adult job.

Gareth's uncle directs films. Gareth, five, has heard of some of the principles involved, and has studied the projector at work at a showing of 'The Wizard of Oz' by the local film society in a memorial hall. Gareth has a very high IQ, a reading age of nine, and great powers of concentration. His father saw him one morning, watching while he put some television storyboards into a black carrier. 'You draw these to get an idea of the film,' his father explained. With no other encouragement, Gareth devoted the whole day to producing 'The Wizard of Oz', pausing briefly for lunch and tea. He drew thirty-five pictures representing key scenes from the film, starting in a single colour and changing into 'technicolor' as the real film does. These he gathered into a sheaf, and stood up on an easel against a white wall. On a table at the other end of the room he placed a projector he had made out of Lego, together with paper 'reels'. The next morning he sat the family down in front of the 'screen', and 'ran' the film, supplying a commentary with musical inter- ludes in the manner of the silent film era.

Gifted children will pick up ideas of this kind, and work on them, provided:

a they bear some relation to what father and/or mother do, or value.

b some help is given with materials.

c the ideas are not over-sold to the children.

d interest is shown and praise given.

The last three points are important. If a child is intelligent, he will soon perceive when he is being fobbed off or got rid of. He will also feel hurt when his productions start becoming taken for granted. It is more important to him that he should be talked with (rather than to) about what he's doing, than be praised for it. But, being human, he values enthusiasm as well as concern.

Teaching, according to some educationists, should be left to teachers. This should be the subject of a much longer book since many parents, and some teachers, believe the job should be shared. Two things are certain. Many experts sincerely believe that teaching a child to read is a job for school. But many gifted children learn to read some time before they go to school. Does this mean that principles should be waived for gifted children?

One answer given by a head teacher with many years' experience of primary schools and of different methods of teaching to read is that a gifted child himself may waive them, but that a parent probably should not. She meant that if a child is determined to copy a brother or sister, or to follow the words as well as the story he is being read, then he will organize it so that he is taught to read. A parent may check whether the interest is really there and continue if it is obvious that the child enjoys it and gets pleasure out of learning. But for a parent to force the pace, or to insist on the child *working at* reading before he is ready to do so, must be wrong. Gifted children often find a way of getting taught to read irrespective of whether their parents are worried about the usual arguments that an early reader will suffer at school when taught a different approach to sounds and words, or when bored while the rest of the class is happily learning. (These arguments are really about teaching methods, *not* about the issue of reading: a teacher who allows children to get confused or bored will find a way of achieving this with a gifted child *whenever* he learns to read.) But gifted children are just like others in that they are not all ready to read at the same age. A child who is obviously very intelligent but making heavy weather of reading should be given more time. Sometimes his emotional ties with his mother make it more difficult to learn something from her in a formal context. A good teacher will not have this problem and will recognize from the child's reactions whether the time is right for a given pace of learning, and whether he has a genuine problem with reading or not. Serious disability, or 'dyslexia', is not unknown in gifted children, and needs special training.

Parents should not make a practice of duplicating school work. But they can always help their children to explore new interests: they can read to them, and they can talk to their children about the world in ways that some might call 'educational'. Visits to museums, exhibitions, airports, concerts; to different kinds of places—a village if you live in a city, a city if you live in the country—and different kinds of events: political demonstrations, sports, archaeological digs. . . . There are so many things that a family can watch or participate in that extend a child's experience and horizons.

There are just a few caveats. Some parents don't know when to stop. Taking a young child into the National Gallery, going into just two rooms, looking at and discussing a few pictures with horses in (or dragons, or battle scenes, etc.) can be very rewarding for parent and child. The child will probably want to go again. But trailing around eighteen rooms, to pile impression on impression, is a waste of time and will put the child off for life. Similarly, doggedly looking for culture in a repetitive way, weekend after weekend, is self-defeating. A gifted child senses when it is an effort, not a genuine enjoyment. *Varying* the kind of excursion you make together is more likely to keep interest high. At some point, a gifted child will probably decide he must, must know a lot more about something. (Bad luck if it's farming and you suffer from hay fever.) He will then want to spend time on farms, following tractors and cows. This may not seem cultural to you—but unless it is very inconvenient, why not let his enthusiasm take its course? For a child under ten, finding out about farming is not necessarily on a different plane from the fine arts. Any child, gifted or not, is liable to appreciate something he can participate in, or copy, more than something which is just there to be studied and admired. Participation brings more enjoyment, greater interest and *deeper learning*, too. Taking a child only to things which he must respect but not touch is like expecting understanding somehow to creep through his skin. It is thoroughly unrealistic. Leaving him solely to the company of pedigree Ayrshires would also be an unrealistic education, but at least he might enjoy it.

Of course choosing a good school, by which I mean an

appropriate school, is an important way in which parents can help a young gifted child. This deserves the following chapter to itself. But once the child is there, taking an interest in the school is crucial. Inevitably where classes are large, teachers understand those children that they hear more about.

Listening to your child talking about the school is just as important. A gifted child will be very imaginative, sometimes, in describing just how horrible a place his school might be. More indicative than lurid accounts is the question of whether the *same* complaints keep coming back. It does not do to badger teachers; if you ask them questions rather than make statements (e.g. 'Do you think Matilda gets a bit bored sometimes?' rather than 'Matilda says she's bored stiff half the time') you achieve the same effect without causing resentment against you or Matilda. Nor does it pay to voice criticisms about the school in front of your child— unless you feel particularly strongly about something which can actually be changed. It doesn't help to make your child feel he is going back every day to an inferior establishment run by a gang of mediocrities. 'I got a shock when Matthew [nine years old, with an IQ of 150] broke into my conversation one day and demanded "If Miss P—— is a flaming idiot, why do I keep having to go to her class? Can't I just stay at home, Mummy?"' This kind of question is unanswerable.

Kellmer Pringle recently made a very thorough study of gifted children who were referred to her unit for assessment because they were not doing well at school. Being able to look at high IQ children who are happy and successful at school as well, she was able to note objectively some ways in which parents influenced achievement. There are of course other points which she indicates as well. But the parental ones are:

_a_ Interest in the child as a person.
_b_ Interest in what the child is doing.
_c_ Interest in education, the child's education, and attitudes towards education.

This can be seen from one angle as drawing a broad distinction between parents who care and those who don't. A young child needs emotional support, a reliable sounding-board for ideas, and a model of attitudes and activity that he admires and respects. Without these at home he will be handicapped unless he is fortunate enough to find them in somebody outside the home. But I would underline another point which is implicit in what Kellmer Pringle declares: that interest in the child _as a person_ is not equivalent to worrying about his school or even stopping to glance over his shoulder to see what he is making. In other terms, it touches on the principle of respect outlined earlier in the chapter, as well as sheer love. A friendly curiosity about what is individual about a gifted child, how he is going to be different from the others in the family, what kind of surprises he will spring, and what individual kind of help he may need—this may mean the difference between applying a superior brain in a functional, mechanical way, and taking pleasure in using one's talents to the full.

Nine
Primary schools for gifted children

What do you want out of a school? If it is simply a question, for you, of making sure that a gifted child gets into the secondary school route that you think is best, the answer is straightforward. Your demands, in fact, are very little different when you are considering a school for a gifted child or for an ordinary child; except, possibly, in the distinctions you feel the gifted child should pick up on his way. You may feel yourself committed to the state system, or the private system, above a certain level.

It is one point of view that, irrespective of the child's intelligence, it makes sense to put him into a prep school so that he can go on to one of the more respected public schools. The view is based on the assumption that where the teachers are paid the most, where the equipment is up to date, where the staff : pupil ratio is favourable, and where the building and grounds are aesthetically pleasing, the best is likely to be done for any child. It may also be based on a feeling that morality, social advantage and career possibilities are inherent in the public school system; these issues can be queried in terms of fact and desirability.

On the other hand you may feel that state education, whatever its merits and demerits in the past, must and will be the education of the future. It may be more desirable for you to risk crowded classrooms and teachers with less distinguished degrees, than to equip your child with an élitist view of society. You may feel antipathetic to what private schooling stands for in your mind. Again, this will affect your attitude to the education of any child.

This is the real background against which particular pluses and minuses about schools have to be considered. This is the moment when basic feelings about state versus private are probably stronger than at any time in the past. The reason is that the transition from a two-tier system of grammar and secondary modern towards comprehensive on the state side has advanced in a patchwork way, and the problems involved in transition have convinced many parents that they cannot rely on the state supplying education that will help their children in the best possible form. These include parents who were educated at grammar schools, alarmed that grammar school teachers do not always continue teaching within a new comprehensive school. They also include parents who were educated at secondary modern schools and who have an idea of offering their children something better than they themselves received.

Many accept that comprehensive education will be best in the long run, but they baulk at risking their own children in helping to set a trend. Gifted children pose a particular problem here.

The tendency has always been, and still is, for gifted children to be siphoned off into private schools. When a parent cannot pay for this, some private schools may be so anxious to have a genuinely gifted child in their ranks that adjustments are made to the fees. Similarly, local authorities will sometimes pay for a gifted child to go to a private school if there seems to be a clear-cut case for providing him with special education that is unavailable locally. This is in fact standard practice for very many local authorities where certain types of handicapped children are concerned, although it is more of a bone of contention if it is for intelligent children. One result of both tendencies is best described in the words of the head teacher of a state primary school in the south of England, whom I approached to talk about gifted children:

Oh, yes. I've met one or two of these, and of course I've read about them. You're talking about those who have a very high IQ or compose music at six. It must be very exciting to have them in your school, and quite a problem too—because I imagine they need very careful handling, and they don't give the teacher an easy ride. We get some very intelligent children, but not the kind you're talking about . . . Actually, there have been one or two, looking back, who've come into our reception class. But they are withdrawn very quickly to go into prep schools. You ought to go to St P— really, or else K— [prep schools]. They've creamed off most of the brightest children around the district. I know the headmaster at St P—, and I'm sure he'll talk to you.

It is remarkable that this is the comment of the head of a primary school. In a comprehensive school, it might be unexceptional. The other remarkable point, however, is that no allowance is made in the head teacher's mind for the possibility that some of her children *might* be gifted, but have not yet made this apparent. Despite the fact that on average, in a given area, only two or three in a hundred children of the same age may be expected to be 'gifted', it must follow that each school with an annual intake of thirty to forty should expect at least one gifted child every other year—*if other things are equal.*

The evidence is that selection, in the sense of creaming off, happens very early in the case of gifted children. Some would argue that this happens with intelligent children in

ut that is beside the point. It is socially undesirable
dness should become associated with divisions in
and that gifted children should acquire experience
of only a limited social setting at school. Indirectly, this
has a result of depressing the attainment level expected of
and gained by children in the state system. For them to
believe they are having a second class education ensures that
social class divisions are perpetuated. The other side of this
coin is the creeping assumption on the part of some
teachers in the state system that they can help their pupils
to go so far, but no further; this may result in a constant
limitation of achievement among some children who may
be gifted which is no less real for not being deliberate. A
reflection of this is the fairly common finding among
children who win awards to universities from state schools
that some of their teachers positively resent their
success.

No comprehensive system will be fully operational in a
way that helps society as a whole, until both the intelligent
and the extremely intelligent child are part of it. But simply
sending them there without adequate provision is to be
doctrinaire just for the sake of it. This is the dilemma we
face now.

A lot is being done to try to provide better opportunities
within the state system for gifted children. These include
enrichment programmes; the provision of teaching materials
which allow individual children to go beyond the basic
syllabus without tying teachers down to giving them disproportionate attention; and the creation of special 'sets'
for pupils with particular flair in a subject to be taught at a
higher or a more intensive level in groups that are drawn
from several classes or even from several schools. These will
be discussed later, as they offer a great deal of hope for the

future. But this chapter will concentrate on the present situation, considering the case of the average parent who knows or suspects his child is gifted and is faced with a choice of schools.

The questions to ask come under seven headings:

1. Has the school got an aim? What are its aims?
Some schools do not appear to have an overall aim: it is left to the individual teacher to supply or not, as he feels fit. The children are kept occupied. Time passes. Some lessons are learnt, some are not: so what? This kind of situation is readily apparent if the head teacher shows lack of concern that you have come to talk to him at all, or that your child should be an individual worth asking questions about. Again, you may only get a blank look when you ask what the main things are that he is looking forward to developing in the school.

Never ask outright what the aim of the school is. As likely as not you will get a meaningless formula such as '. . . to produce Christian gentlemen' or, '. . . to help girls take their rightful place in the world'.

'Do children enjoy it here, do you feel?' is not a bad question to ask. Not that it will be answered with great accuracy, but simply to see what the reaction is. Sheer surprise at the question, or something like 'Oh yes. When they're occupied, they're happy,' may well indicate that you are visiting a public school entrance sausage-machine. Here, your gifted child stands a very good chance of getting into the public school of your choice. But the gifted creative child may have a hard time of it. And the high IQ child who conforms and shines may end up just that much more restricted in his views on what learning is actually for. A naturally competitive child may be in his element— although it may not make him more lovable. It might stimulate him more than an entirely permissive school which avoids putting any kind of pressure on its pupils.

Ideally, the aims should be to help each child make the most of himself while encouraging him to enjoy helping others as well as competing with them. This means giving him a clear view of other interests, and the community's interests, as well as developing his own particular talents.

At all events, the aims should not be inconsistent with the gifted child being stimulated to stretch himself (as opposed to just fulfilling a stint), to take up new interests, and to explore new ways of working. A school which devotes itself to raising the average performance of the average may be the wrong place for him.

2. *Are the teachers graduates?*
Some of the best teachers are not graduates: they just teach well. But a *gifted* child will start asking questions that perplex those whose general knowledge is ample enough for most clever children. The teacher without in-depth understanding of a subject may resent the questioner as a threat; or he may choose to laugh at him or ignore him. The best teacher knows a lot, but admits when he doesn't know something, saying, 'Let's look it up in a book together at the end of the lesson.' An example of this may help to show what to look for at a school:

Bill showed he was brilliant at mathematics when he was six (not just good—brilliant). His teacher at primary school thought quadratic equations might amuse him. And so they did. But she suddenly realized, to her alarm, that her memory of how they work was faulty. 'Will you please go over this with me, Bill,' she said, turning to a page in a text book, 'so that we can help each other work it out?' This suggestion that they should learn together apparently melted Bill's heart completely, and cemented their relationship. In a higher class, he would sometimes slip away and seek her out, hoping to renew it for a while. She always showed interest in the new ground he was breaking, and listened carefully when he explained elementary calculus to her. With the head teacher she got in touch with a maths don at Oxford, who was able to comment on Bill's work by correspondence, suggesting ways of helping. And this is an example of just what a gifted child can do with.

3. Are the subjects in tight compartments?

Few children develop evenly in all subjects. The gifted child may, of course, be a natural all-rounder. But many have a problem which can lead to their being thought incapable in a particular subject. Where subjects are not taught as separate disciplines at the primary stages, a gifted child can be helped to gain confidence in one he finds baffling by attacking it from a side where he already has some mastery.

Bill, the boy mentioned above, was less happy with reading than other work. He was not *bad* at it, but he made heavy weather of it. His teacher offered him a book on the lives of mathematicians, which was designed for children aged about twelve. She sat down with him, started him off and awoke his interest. Satisfied, she left him to it. Bill approached other children to help him with words he could not get straight away. He took the book home and got his parents to help him. In three days, he had greedily wolfed it all down.

Some children, even gifted children, have problems with learning 'series'. (If you suddenly ask one to tell you the names of the months in order starting from March, they may reveal their problem.) These can be helped a great deal by merging subjects—for example, by expressing number problems verbally, or by relating historical sequence to events, types of people, buildings, etc. For a creative child this approach may make a dreary area suddenly seem alive with possibilities, because he can contribute to it more easily.

4. How competitive is the school?
As implied above, some gifted children do seem naturally competitive. They enjoy comparing marks and happily chew over form placings even when they are not on top. Cricket averages or league tables have a similar fascination for some very clever children, even though their skill at the game may be limited to fantasy. Girls are quite as likely to be fierce competitors as are boys, at least at primary school. (Some psychologists argue that they care less, however, when they lose.)

Not all gifted children are dyed-in-the-wool competitors, however, and in a society where co-operation is valued, and the study of how people work happily and productively together may have been under-valued historically, it seems a shame to make a gifted child believe that demonstrating that he is better is all-important. The amount of competitive spirit should be explored by a parent, who has then to judge how far this suits the personality of the child. The more creative the child is, the less competition will attract him—probably because he asks himself 'Why the fuss?' Extremes of competitiveness cannot be good for any child. Here is a conversation between the parents of a seven-year-old French girl which may illustrate this point:

'She's not so very clever, you know. I believe her assessment was wrong.'
'I think she's clever. After all, she came sixth out of twenty-three this summer, and was top in her composition.'
'Maybe she's a bit lazy . . .'

If your child is at a very competitive school, it will n
him if the atmosphere of the parade ring is extend
the afternoons and weekends at home. Demanding of a gifted
child why he is not top of the class seems excessive
pressure. At best it is asking for revolt.

5. Are there opportunities for the individual?
This is several questions in one. First, does the school
organize itself to suit its own convenience, or does it allow
an element of compromise? Once a child gets through the
task set for the whole class, or completes the syllabus, what
happens then? Does he just revise, or get a book out of the
library? What if he is musical, or a promising sculptor?
Must he give up lessons of this kind when the whole class is
expected to go on to a second language?

A very important aspect of this problem is whether
children are made to re-learn, according to the school's
approved method, what they (and particularly a gifted
child) may have already picked up at home. Learning a
second method of reading is totally unnecessary and unkind.

Nobody can expect a school to be tailored to his child.
But this should be a matter of degree, where negotiation is
possible. The best clue as to how flexible a school may be is
found by talking to other parents, since a great deal depends
on individual teachers, rather than the head's polite reply.

6. Does the school accelerate clever children?
The easiest arrangement, from an academic point of view,
is to move a child who seems to be in advance of the rest of
his class to the class immediately above. This is known as
'acceleration'. The problem is that although the child is
now working at a level which may be more appropriate, he
is faced with several emotional problems: he has to make
new friends in an atmosphere which may be unfriendly, and

even hostile, with children who are older. These children may be emotionally and socially more mature. When confronted with a new arrival who has a lower tears threshold, they may regard him as a 'little squit' who has no business with them. The youngest child in a class is often under pressure to prove that he has a right to be there. He senses that others are questioning this right and becomes more nervous about his work. He may also be too young, emotionally, for the length of homework that may be expected in a higher class, and at the same time misses out on lessons like art which he enjoyed, but which are not considered serious enough for the higher class. Some children enjoy the thrill of being accelerated and feel pride at being the baby of the form. But the demands on them are now recognized to be far greater than was once thought.

A school with an automatic procedure for acceleration must be suspect. There are other answers to the question of how to keep up a gifted child's interest and stretch his mind. One is to arrange 'sets', so that for part of the day he is working with older children, while most of the time he remains in the same class as those of his age group. This means he can get the glory of moving up while enjoying the security of staying put. Another means is to supply extra sessions for gifted children (in something they are really interested in) to work in a science lab or some other place which is associated with higher learning, under the eye of student teachers or volunteers from the regular staff. The idea here is to 'enrich' the education of those who are intelligent and interested enough to profit from sessions that are parallel to syllabus work. There are schools which believe in 'feeding the environment' so that gifted children, while remaining with those of their age group, are trained to develop their work further *by themselves*; this means that the teachers *start* by being able to provide opportunities for any child who shows he can use them.

7. *Does the school 'stream' the children? How rigid is the streaming?*
At some prep schools children are told bluntly, at nine or so, that: 'We believe that you, Richards, are scholarship material. But you, Williams, are moving into 5B because you will be lucky to get common entrance.' Whether this is part of a psychological ploy or not (e.g. to get Williams to work harder) it is a kind of division that makes a long-lasting impression on children. If Richards is gifted, he will see himself as programmed for the educational élite, and Williams will resent his success, perhaps compensating by deriding any study that goes beyond the bounds of the strictly necessary as 'swotting'.

The degree of streaming is a question of the school's flexibility. How much likelihood is there of a child switching from one level to another? Do the children feel they have been given a fixed educational tag? Sets drawn from classes that are based on age can bypass the need for streaming, and the psychological compartmentalization that can follow. The French term for a stream at school is 'couloir'; this implies a fixed pattern of progress along one or other of the corridors, and much experiment in French education aims at breaking the rigidity of this.

In the extreme (but not rare) case of Richards and Williams quoted above, the IQ levels may in fact have been opposite to what their teacher thought. If Richards were intelligent, but not *so* intelligent, he might be subjected to expectations that he could not fulfil. Williams might be the gifted child but, for some of the reasons discussed elsewhere in this book, he has never shone. Being addressed as doubtful common entrance material is only likely to confirm him in his belief that his habit of doing no more than his stint is soundly based. Or, depending on his personality, it may encourage him to believe that school is an overrated institution where he meets nothing but misunderstanding.

*   *   *

Two findings from research among gifted children are worth mentioning here. One, that at primary level teachers cannot always pick out the gifted children, is relevant to the argument against rigid streaming. The second has more general significance. In his book on the Brentwood Experiment, S. A. Bridges draws attention to the fact that many gifted children who were chosen from neighbouring schools for 'enrichment' sessions one afternoon a week, had a strong sense of 'stint'. This is typified by the question 'How many pages should we write, miss?'

There are several ways in which schools will encourage a sense of stint, even among gifted children. One is to give long homework exercises, in several subjects every evening, to children who are too young to organize their own time in a systematic way. In order to survive this regime, it is natural for a child to learn to submerge his curiosity about what a subject holds and acquire a feeling for the amount of work he can get away with producing, while maintaining a good position. Clearly the more intelligent the child, the more accurate and successful he will become at this. Being given school work to do as punishment, and associating detention in school with punishment, contribute to this. Other factors contribute to the stint, too, which have little to do with the school—anxiety to retain links and friendship with less academic children is one. But it is the school, in the shape of teachers who have a good record for stimulating interest and enthusiasm and in respect of the time they have to provide individual attention, that bears the prime responsibility for keeping the sense of stint low.

One important point is varying the diet. Gifted or not, a child must get bored sometimes. The skill is to anticipate this boredom, by communicating that a subject had now best be left to tomorrow, and going on to something else. It takes imagination, rather than magnificent new equipment, to provide a rich diet. Despite reservations that many have about the Victorian ideal of a sound mind in a sound body, games must have a part to play in this diet. I take games here in the widest sense, since their importance seems to be primarily in letting a child run free, work off frustrations and use up his surplus energy. This can be done in groups or by individuals.

Over-organization of games is self-defeating for several reasons. With any child, substituting one tight discipline for another effectively prevents letting off steam in a natural way. A gifted child is often critical of team games, either when they appear to him to be too puerile to devote serious time and energy to them, or when they offer no opportunity for him to shine at them. A school which offers alternative sports for children who are more individualist may be that much more suitable for a gifted child. It is a long time since Terman's research disproved the widely held belief that highly intelligent children are necessarily unathletic. But recognition that different kinds of temperament find pleasure in team and individual sport, in competitive and non-competitive ways of using energy, has been delayed at a number of schools.

Once a good school is found, of course it has to be watched. The morale and the teaching methods at a school change very rapidly with staff turnover. Similarly, how your child fits in to it, and what he derives from it, will change too. Reassessment—without disturbing the child's faith in it —is important. Progress is never even, whatever the school or the child. But a gifted child may outgrow his environment more quickly than others.

Ten
Who helps the gifted child?

Those teachers and educationists who deny the existence of
gifted children (or who assume that they never happen in
their school) have been on the decline over the past ten years.
This is partly the result of greater publicity given to them
and to what happens to them. But there is still a body of
opinion that is opposed to spending money or time on
gifted children, or doing anything which distinguishes
them in their own eyes, or in the eyes of other children. The
arguments put forward here divide into two. First, there is
the case that they do not *need* special help—'if they are so
clever,' as one has put it, 'they will shine wherever they are'.
Second, there is the feeling that, for their sakes and for
society's, it is mistaken to draw attention to them. Fortunately, this view is beginning to decline too. I hope that I
have given sufficient reason why this is desirable.

While the long struggle involved in the changing of
official attitudes proceeds, it is important that parents
should know what is being done and in what quarters to
help them.

The work of the National Association for Gifted Children
(NAGC) deserves special mention. It was set up by a small
group of individuals who were concerned about the happiness and the prospects of gifted children who demonstrably
do *not* 'shine wherever they are'. Their early struggles have
been well described by Margaret Branch, one of the founders,
in her book on gifted children.

Henry Collis, the director of the NAGC, is anxious to make it clear that the first priority of the organization is the improvement in the happiness and welfare of gifted children themselves. Through that, the aim is to help parents and society as a whole. But the emphasis is on advantage to the children, not on the 'exploitation of our natural resources of brain power'. Helping gifted children towards achievements that make a big contribution to our arts and our technology should not be inconsistent with this policy. But it is easy to think of ways in which the gifted might be pushed towards this goal without regard for their well-being.

He also stresses a desire to avoid steps which could directly or indirectly lead towards their becoming an élite split off either mentally or physically from others. To help these children to be integrated in their families, at school and in society, however, depends on their attaining a sense of fulfilment and avoiding a sense of frustration and grudge.

The NAGC is organized on a national and local basis. It has not been possible to start up a local group in every area. Any parents who contact them may find that there is, in fact, a ready-made local group to join, or that the association intends to start one when there are sufficient members in the district.

The services provided by the NAGC cover a wide range. In certain cases they advise parents who approach them to arrange for an accurate, objective assessment to be made of their child's IQ. This is done through the School Psychological Service but can be arranged privately. As a number of the children whose parents come forward show signs of disturbance or complain of problems at school (parents of gifted children who are progressing perfectly satisfactorily have less of an incentive to come forward) it makes sense that IQ assessment should be made by an expert who has a thorough knowledge of child psychology. An analysis of possible reasons for problems appearing, in terms of emotional immaturity, etc., can then be made at the same time. It is unrealistic to expect that everything will become apparent at the interview. But at least a foundation of objective assessment is laid.

Not all parents who have their child assessed, however certain they may be of the outcome, will find their beliefs and wishes confirmed. But it must be better to learn this and to have realistic expectations than to wonder why a child does not display brilliant progress.

Parents who have been surprised or alarmed by their experience with unusual children derive strength from meeting others with similar experience. It is reassuring to find that the problems and wrangles they have encountered are not unique and have not necessarily been occasioned by their personal shortcomings as parents. From another point of view it is often salutary for parents of a gifted child, whom they may consider to be the most significant arrival in learning since the young Goethe, to discover that he *has* got equals who show every bit as much promise. For these reasons, local branches of the NAGC provide a forum in which parents can talk to each other, and share their feelings.

On an informal basis, the NAGC can discuss with parents recent experiences that others have had with particular schools or particular types of school. This is *not*, however, a comprehensive advisory service: local educational advisers, who *may* belong to the NAGC, are often in the best position to advise on local schools and how they might suit particular children. The NAGC does, however, have a professional consulting service which is free to members.

A *Children*. Activities Days are organized for parents' benefit as well as for children. But the primary function is to give children who are gifted a chance to meet and be stimulated by each other; to join in activities which are pitched at a higher intellectual level than they are likely to meet ordinarily; and to encounter new ideas, presented in a way which can kindle the enthusiasm to tackle them seriously at home. Formal teaching, as at school, is generally avoided. For example, there would not be an English lesson as such, but the children opting for this activity might be shown how to produce a play; no music lesson either—but a chance for young composers to try out what they have been developing on a captive and attentive audience. There is a mixture of the sedentary and the active: at a recent NAGC Activities Day in Hertfordshire, the children could choose à la carte from a list of possibilities: drama, pottery, football, chess, physics, origami or watching a zoologist demonstrate a range of animals brought in specially for the purpose.

Another kind of 'Day' that the NAGC branch may organize in an area is one for specialists in a particular field: for young musicians, for young scientists, or perhaps for those who want to make puppets, write a play, make the scenery and present it in the evening. One comment sometimes made about these children in school is that they are impatient with the others they are supposed to be collaborating with on a project, and this attitude is then criticized for being élitist rather than simply impatient. The opportunity to be active with others who are as quick-thinking and imaginative as they are is a useful extension of their experience in co-operation.

For all activities the children are called 'explorers' and there is a special week for forty of them each year at Windmill House in Warwickshire during August.

At most of these occasions brothers and sisters are

welcome too. This depends on the number of pl[...]
able, and to some extent the activity involved,
recognized that splitting a family in the name of [...]
is likely to be bad policy.

B *Teachers.* The more teachers learn about gifted children, the
more they are likely to watch out for them in the classroom.
They will then recognize the possibility of giftedness, even
among some who are achieving little, and know how to be
helpful to them without destroying the balance of attention
in the class. They will also be more willing and less
suspicious about children being assessed independently,
when the case for this special attention arises.

Teachers who have helped gifted children in schools have
often represented a kind of sporadic, unco-ordinated effort
—despite their excellent work. Gifted children—and indeed
(simply) children—are best aided by teachers working
systematically and in harmony with the whole school.

The NAGC has organized seminars for teachers and
head teachers, and it has pressed for information about the
subject to be included in the basic syllabus at teachers'
training colleges.

C *Department of Education and Science.* While the NAGC is recognized by this Government Department, it is worth noting
that the DES itself does not claim to have an official policy
on gifted children or their education. Much educational
policy is decided at local level, and therefore this is not to be
expected. However, the DES can and does observe, take note,
encourage experimental projects and organize discussions
or working parties to get a better understanding of the issue
at all levels. Where it can make its views definite is on
questions of the practicality or the funding of this or that
scheme. As it does this on a wide range of issues, it is

dependent on listening to advice from outside its walls on which issues deserve more, and which less, attention. The public voice is a considerable factor in determining department concern, but that is not the same thing as determining policy. That is much more a local matter.

In the summer of 1973, the DES held their first open course on the teaching of gifted children in primary and middle schools. It took place at Brighton College of Education, and most of those responsible for major research in that area were able to inform each other and discuss the future. The DES has also accepted that two schools which provide very specialized help for gifted children—the Yehudi Menuhin School for young musicians and the Royal Ballet School—should be aided by direct grant. This does suggest that while the official concern of the DES for both slow and fast learners lies in improving the education of as many children as possible 'in situ'—that is, at the local school to which most of the local children go—there is recognition that some gifted children may need to have their particular talents developed elsewhere, in a special school.

D *Local Education Authorities.* The NAGC seminars are sometimes geared towards LEAs as well as teachers. It is fair to say that many take a more active interest in gifted children's welfare and education at least partly as a result of this influence. Others are less receptive. Some Education Officers find that their recommendations for helping gifted children, because they do not seem in accord with the principle of fair shares for all, are turned down by the authority as a whole.

But, in the end, local authorities are always concerned about current feeling in their area. When they sense greater concern for geriatric cases, they spend more time and money on improving relevant services; where there are outcries about the plight of handicapped children, these get a bigger share of the cake. The NAGC task, then, is to influence public opinion at large by drawing the attention of a large number of people to gifted children, explaining why they should be helped and what can be done to help them.

One Education Officer at the Brighton course in summer 1973 said:

I've been trying for some time now to get my authority to approve my plan to organize enrichment sessions for gifted children in my area. The trouble is that the principle is politically unacceptable to them. But I have found that they are receptive to the idea of spending money and sparing school building space to provide a centre for activities designed to help children with special problems. In theory, I have to wait, then, for more gifted children to be identified, and to give evidence of disturbance, *before* actually stepping in. However, it may be possible to start something for a few very clever children with emotional problems and build on that. It must help, I am sure, if I avoid all mention of 'gifted'. Some name like 'exceptional children' would be less likely to arouse antagonism.

This illustrates two of the problems faced by the NAGC, and by anybody who is trying to help these children: the fact that it is only when things go wrong with them that they evoke sympathy on any scale, and the defensive attitude encountered when the word 'gifted' is used. An alternative word is not easy to find, without being misleading. 'Exceptional' has been suggested, but in the United States this is often used to mean mentally handicapped, and confusion between the two is undesirable. A term like 'frustration-risk children' might be more to the point, in that it indicates one strong reason for helping them. It puts the burden on society to give them opportunities to find fulfilment.

If there is to be less antagonism and more positive action on behalf of these children, it must become more possible for them to be spotted and encouraged among poorer families. This depends on developing a sensitive and comprehensive detection system across society. Some psychologists attached to education departments are anxious to increase the business of searching for 'target population groups' among local schools. This means screening new intakes of children into primary schools (and, if possible, at nursery groups or schools) in order to spot those who are likely to belong to groups known to need and benefit from special training. For example, finding out that a child is well below average in intelligence but with a certain potential in, say, mechanical work, gives one the chance to spare him the uphill struggle of competing and trying to catch up in an ordinary school. He may need to go into a special unit in an ordinary school, or to an ESN school, until he gives signs of being able to take a transfer in his stride. If a gifted child is spotted early on he too can be helped, by whatever means seem most appropriate to his talents and his maturity.

But the principle of catching them young is barely developed in this country. 'An educational psychologist like myself,' complained one, 'is always forced to *react* to a crisis in a child's life. I cannot work to a preventive strategy, so as to anticipate a crisis likely to occur.' This is changing—but slowly.

Screening can help children most when there are clearly defined ways and means of supplying the right kind of education for their handicap, whether this be giftedness or slow learning. Developing 'prescription education' in this way will make screening fruitful.

Other bodies who are helping gifted children are based at universities and colleges. These are education departments and centres for training teachers which devote part of their energies to running enrichment sessions. An example of pioneer work of this kind is the Brentwood Experiment referred to earlier. At Bristol University Dr Bill Wilks has been arranging opportunities for enrichment on similar lines for some years now.

Wilks has noted one particular advantage of this system: the fact that children can, in these circumstances, try out something that has been brewing at the back of their minds but which they have not been able to attempt either at school or at home. In a physics lab at the Centre for Science Education at Bristol, during the course of an afternoon, I saw four children aged eleven and twelve engaged in:

a experiments with a ripple tank, studying light patterns.
b making glass beads of different colours.
c joining together components to make a transistor radio.

The first two activities had been suggested by student teachers and enthusiastically received. The third was the spontaneous work of a boy who had made 'several radios' at home but had very much wanted to try out this particular design he had in mind, which needed special equipment.

A line had to be drawn, in fact, in the case of another boy attending the Bristol sessions. He arrived at the physics lab with a bulging notebook. 'I want to make this machine I've invented,' he announced, 'which will have perpetual motion.' The student teachers spent a long time discussing it. There were several novel features in the design, and they were—to put it mildly—impressed. 'It would be very interesting to do'—they broke the news gently—'but very, very, expensive.'

A typical Wednesday afternoon at Bristol is split into two halves. The activities vary from year to year, according to the subjects of the student teachers who volunteer to help. The children are recommended by their head teachers. Some are delivered, some collected. Half the time a child might spend doing drama, mathematics, or something in the Science Centre. The second half, after a break, might be devoted to Greek, geography or art.

The most striking thing about the sessions is the way in which the children seem intensely but happily involved in what they are doing. Clearing up is often protracted, because they are anxious to see their work reach a natural conclusion. In the course of this, it is noticeable that they have a very easy-going relationship with the student teachers. These seemed more like partners, or older brothers and sisters, than teachers. This atmosphere seemed as important as the fact of individual attention, or the availability of special equipment.

'I was dead nervous of these kids at first,' admitted one student teacher. 'Especially M—, because you just couldn't tell what he knows and what he doesn't know. But once you see they're interested in something, you tell them what you can, and find out about the rest together.' A simple approach, but effective.

The ability of a gifted child to respond sensibly and seriously to an adult-to-adult manner is often surprising, because it happens at such a young age. It depends on the real adult having something interesting to offer quite naturally. And it can mislead people into thinking that the gifted child is always like that. In fact, a number of them are emotionally incapable of keeping it up for very long. Those involved with the Brentwood Experiment stressed the value of arranging that there should be a break during which 'they can really let their hair down'. It was interesting to note how the children at Bristol relaxed over lemonade and buns to the point of repeating typical school jokes to each other.

Other opportunities for gifted children with specific talents to concentrate on their particular bent include orchestral weeks, sometimes organized by music colleges and sometimes by local authorities where musical interest and achievement are high. At Harrow, near London, the current practice is for two orchestral weeks to be fixed up each year. For four days, during school holidays, children recommended by their teachers for showing unusual promise on orchestral instruments are put through an intensive course leading up to a concert on Thursday evening. Professional musicians and music teachers are in charge.

The degree of enthusiasm for this is best illustrated by Louise, a girl cellist aged nine, who spent the first day studying the music for the concert within a string group, practising hard, and enjoying one short break for lunch and another for a spell of netball. Late in the afternoon, there was an hour and a half's rehearsal of the full orchestra, under a professional conductor. He was used to displays of artistic temperament, but was taken aback by the way his hands were seized after the rehearsal and a voice shaking with emotion cried up to him 'Thank you! Oh, thank you! It was all so wonderful!' In fact, it had been starting, stopping, trying again, and the inevitable 'Back to bar 36, and come in when I say!' But it was a revelation. It showed Louise how exciting playing in combination, rather than just as a budding soloist, can be. And it gave insight into the delight of getting down to work in music in a committed, almost professional way. At the end of the week Louise was exhausted but still participating, in her mind, in the successful concert which had crowned it.

This kind of experience seems particularly important where children who are artistically talented are concerned. They sense what it could be like to be in a group who are dedicated to understanding, or reproducing, or creating something in the arts. They may develop their own technique endlessly—whatever it is—but unless they have the opportunity to join in with others, either to prepare a concert, to make a film or a play, or to design a frieze or a mural, they are detached in their development. All those theatre groups which arrange for sessions in drama or expression for children can provide this opportunity, if it is organized in a way that does not lose the gifted child's respect.

Another example is a very bold experiment backed by the Inner London Education Authority. A group of children who are musically very gifted have been selected from a large number of primary schools within striking distance of Pimlico Comprehensive School, in London. These children spend most of their day with their separate classes, but miss a few periods a week in order to have special music instruction, both separately and together. Because it is an officially sponsored scheme, due care would be taken to include those children who show exceptional promise, to support it with suitable rooms and all the necessary equip- and to attract the best teachers for the job. By September 1973 there were forty-five of these children. Some of the more advanced are members of the London Schools Symphony Orchestra, and have toured with it giving concerts in England and abroad. As well as stimulating other children to take up music successfully, they seem to have enriched the general interest in the arts. But this experiment is only recent, and needs careful evaluation. It may be fair to claim simply that it has opened a door for some children with musical promise to make a serious study of it, and see how far they are suited to this without being uprooted.

It is easy to see how the principle of the Pimlico Experiment might be adapted to help children in other areas, possibly with other talents. There is nothing as yet comparable for those who seem to have a genuine linguistic gift, for example, or a mathematical one. Young sportsmen, by contrast (provided theirs is a 'mainstream' sport), can take advantage of training schemes run by sporting clubs, or by branches of the National Sports Council.

Some who have studied this area have a rather sad conviction that much of the effort to help gifted children comes too late. That is, help is forthcoming for those who have been selected, which is partly a function of middle-class environment. This is not entirely true, but it has a basis in truth. Recognizing the fact that many children in poorer families who may be gifted are never given sufficient encouragement to be recognized for what they are, the NAGC has made contact with health officers at local level, and with the Department of Health and Social Security as well.

The aim is to encourage the first objective observers of any child, that is the doctors at mother and baby clinics, and official health visitors, to look for signs of unusually fast mental development, just as they have been trained over the years to take more and more notice of unusually slow progress. The counterpart to this is watching for indications of something going wrong between parents and child which could have its origin in high intelligence. The value of this observation is that when a health visitor notes very early eye focusing, and early mastery of movements that demand good co-ordination, plus a very active curiosity, etc., she can prepare the mother for what may lie ahead. This does not mean announcing 'You have a gifted baby, Mrs Jones. Congratulations!' It may mean saying, 'He is a very alert little chap, isn't he? You know, I don't often come across them quite so advanced. What you may find is that he needs less sleep than most other young children. He could be obstinate, too, because he'll want to know why he shouldn't do something, rather than just follow orders . . .' This means preparing the parents for what may be rather like a meaningless struggle if they expect him to sleep normal hours, and sit still while he is entertained with biscuits and pop records. Gradually (assuming the original signs were correctly read) the news may be broken that the child is very intelligent. Talking in terms of 'gifted' may be premature and unwise; indeed, to a later generation it may seem the wrong word entirely. This forewarning, however, prevents a situation where parents without a tradition of achievement in intellectual work in their families become less and less enthusiastic about a child who just seems difficult. It should avoid going overboard on early diagnosis too.

Work of this kind could have a big part to play in reducing the divisions in society that equate learning and advancement of many kinds with social class advantage. It is still very much an idea, rather than a policy or practice.

Eleven
Schooling for life

At some stage, parents have to say to themselves, 'Well, that looks like being John's schooling. That will take him up to college (or wherever) if all goes well.' Sometimes a decision on his entire programme will be taken very early in his life: he may be entered into a school with several sections to it, which sees him through 'from the cradle to the grave'. Or, he may be put into the state system on the assumption that this will be perfectly adequate, or on the basis that nothing else can be afforded anyway. But even in these cases there are moments when something jolts a parent—their child's attitude, impressions of the teachers, or a sense of missed opportunity—to make him reappraise the situation. Reappraisal (provided it doesn't happen every week) makes sense. After all, a child has only one school life to lead.

Gifted children pose a particular problem, especially when their gift is highly specialized. Here is a comparison of two gifted children in the same family—both of whom are exceptionally talented in music. Their fortunes in education reflect problems of other gifted children with different, but specialized talents.

Gordon had a very marked response to music when he was in his cot. Certain tunes, whether played or sung, would make him jog up and down with huge delight. One Schubert song affected him in particular. At two, he probed for tunes on a piano keyboard. He did not convince his parents, however, that he was interested or musical enough to have any formal teaching until he was five. Thereafter, his progress was rapid. He commanded a great deal of attention with his piano playing by the time he was ten, and a basic dilemma confronted his parents. Should Gordon have a normal, general education (with the risk that pressure of work in other subjects would rob him of the practice time and experience of playing in groups that he needed to become a good musician); or, should he be given a cursory general education, with his time and efforts directed mainly towards music? This dilemma is very common. Where the parents are musicians (bearing in mind they have had experience in their lives of others who have not quite made the grade as performers) the dilemma seems no less difficult than in the case of Gordon's parents, who enjoy music but do not live by it.

By coincidence, a specialist school for young musicians was about to open. Gordon became one of the first intake of fifteen pupils, chosen with extreme care from many applicants. The school was different then from what it is now. The first pupils were boarded in a hotel: now it flourishes in a huge estate with beautiful grounds. What has persisted is a very high standard of music teaching and a concern that every child should be helped as much as possible to fulfil musical ambitions.

Gordon was unhappy at first but flourished later, after the move to Surrey, and after the advent of the present headmaster. In his last years at the school, Gordon feels there was an excellent balance between ordinary academic teaching, music, and recreation. The best thing, in his estimate, was 'being able to get to hear really good performers: I might not have got to hear Michelangeli if I hadn't been at the school'.

He has his criticisms, too. These are made by a single ex-pupil, and so cannot be regarded as representative opinion. They are given here not to attack the school but to illustrate points of difficulty about teaching gifted children.

There is far more attention paid to gifted soloists: not everybody got the same chance to play in front of an audience. They had little time for my interest in composing—the accent was so much on producing performers. When I left, I had a strange sense of disorientation. I think a number of my friends there had it too. You don't know exactly what to do when you leave. You've been in a world with enclosed grounds, exam dates and other targets, and close supervision. It's not just because it's a boarding school. It's the concentration on music too. It's a different world outside.

Whether the criticism is justified is irrelevant. The points to be noted are:

1. Gordon was gifted, but divergent—in contrast with some of the other children there. He determinedly pursued a composer's, not a performer's, career. (He is still doing so.) Even in a specialist school, a gifted child can show himself to be more specialist than the specialists have allowed for. When looking at different schools this possibility is an important one to consider.

2. The smaller its link with real life as most people know it, the less of a preparation for the outside world a school is going to be. If there is little question that a child is going to continue living most of his life in a musical milieu—fine. Otherwise, steps have to be taken to ensure that a child learns about other kinds of people and other kinds of life, and the holidays may need to be planned with this in mind.

157

Philippa, his sister, also showed a great interest in music. Her education was entirely different. She was competitive with her brother, but progressed more slowly at the piano, since she was not a 'self-starter' at practising. About the age of nine, she persuaded the local church organist to let her try out his instrument, and has largely neglected the piano as a result. She also longed to play the oboe, and for a few very frustrating years she had to make do with recorders. Her interests were at a tangent to those pursued at Gordon's school. After an audition-interview (at nine), her parents were informed that she was 'very musical', but that they had no place for her. A possibility was to consider other music schools, but she expressed sudden reluctance to board.

Her parents decided that a comprehensive school in process of restructure in a nearby town would be a good place for her. The forte at this school was to be its artistic side—including anything to do with music, drama, painting, sculpture, batik, and so on. In addition to a basic, broad education the children were to be given every chance to show what kind of artistic talents they might have, and to enjoy developing them. Discussion with the headmaster and the local authority led to everyone agreeing that although technically Philippa was outside the catchment area, she ought to flourish at the school.

And so she did, from the age of twelve to fourteen. The head and most of the senior staff took a lot of interest in her, as they seemed to do in all the children. She was given help and encouragement with the organ, and a good oboe was obtained for her to have a trial run before her family bought one for her to keep. While her need to practise and have instruction was respected, she was drawn into a lot of other activities, too. She showed promise at acting, and was given an exacting part to play by the local repertory company.

Her parents noted with some satisfaction that she was moving ahead more quickly in subjects like mathematics and English than her brother. Everything, in fact, seemed to be moving favourably for Philippa, and her parents felt that this state school might indeed be better than the specialist school for musically gifted children.

A change of headmaster need not mean a complete change. But it did for Philippa. The new head at her school proclaimed an end to pressure of any kind. Everyone, teachers and pupils alike, were to clasp hands and be friends, dipping into a class for work every now and then only if they really had the urge. The first to suffer was the school orchestra which had been, by all accounts, remarkably good. It capsized, and only the keenest—in twos and threes—carried on the musical tradition. Teachers left to go to other schools, while only those who were happy in an entirely laissez-faire system remained, or joined.

Philippa describes the transition like this:

They abandoned the school uniform. This made it go down a lot. Where everyone had worked before, now they did what they liked. Drugs came in. The head wanted to get in with the druggies. (Int.: Who do you mean?) The people at school who did *nothing* except drinking and drugs. Their problem was coming from rich homes. I enjoyed the first two years there, because the music was so good. Anyway, my 'O' level results got terribly bad, and I left. The orchestra is virtually non-existent now.

It should be said at once that this transition might just as easily have struck a private school. It is also possible that for *some* children it may have been satisfactory, and even (though I doubt it) beneficial. But a gifted child can be very resentful of a sense of sluggishness, of not being stretched. And it is a parent's task to observe whether this kind of frustration is creeping in.

Both Gordon and Philippa ended up at music academies. The routes they took could not have been more different. They have different experience, different kinds of friends, and although both of them had struggles, these were of different character. Gordon's struggle to pursue what he wanted, as opposed to competing to be a virtuoso pianist, was in a tightly knit world. Philippa's fight to progress was in a much more open society, where the pressure against her was to conform to a work-shy dilettante model, and there was no sense of dedication.

If one knew more about a school before making a decision, it would be easier to match the school and the likely struggles to a child's personality. This is rarely possible without an up-to-date knowledge of other parents' experiences with gifted children of various kinds, at various schools. This is an indirect benefit of being in the NAGC, where such discussions are possible.

With gifted children, the likelihood of thinking in terms of boarding school must be greater—simply because the chances of dissatisfaction with what is locally available must be higher. This raises a serious problem, where children are emotionally unequipped for the transition from home to dormitory. It has already been argued that emotional maturity may take a long time to catch up with intellectual advances. Some boarding schools are particularly good about bothering to notice whether a young entrant is happy or eating his heart out—others assume that 'they all muddle through in the end'. If contemplating boarding, it is very important to consider which kind of boarding school your child is capable of fitting into, and then to assess schools by this criterion as well.

Contact with children of all kinds is a fine i
comprehensive school, in its perfect form, shoul
this, with children drawn from all socio-econom.
and all levels of ability. Different interests should be represented there, too, so that new ideas have the greatest chance
of circulation. If a gifted child could concentrate on his
particular skills and interests, and be stretched in them, as
well as enjoying such a varied atmosphere, he would be
educated in a way appropriate to his intelligence without
taking a narrow view of the world. But how can this be
arranged, when:

a the big priority in comprehensives is to upgrade the
   average result?
b the intellectual quality of a comprehensive starts at a
   disadvantage because of creaming off, and also
   because of the resultant habit that teachers develop of
   thinking first and foremost (if not exclusively) in terms
   of average standard?

This shows why comprehensive education is not going to be
attractive to parents of gifted children until they see
evidence of corrective measures being taken. This is why
projects such as the Pimlico Experiment described earlier are
so important. These constitute *evidence* for the claim that
comprehensive schools cater for children of all abilities.
Evidence is going to be more important to parents as time
goes on. The kind of answer exemplified by the ILEA comment in 1973 to parents planning to start their own school
rather than accept the placements their children were given
cuts no ice where gifted children are concerned. This comment was: 'There is no such thing as a bad school in
London.' This is like claiming that all teachers give the same
lessons.

There are two further issues, which are difficult to disentangle. The first is how to combine specialized tuition with the basic routine of an ordinary secondary school. The second is that children who are very intelligent and have a particular bent derive pleasure and benefit from being with similar children. There may not be many such at an ordinary secondary school. Both considerations provoke the question —how big a specialist dose should the child get?

The violinist, according to several famous violinists, needs to master the basic techniques at a very early age: therefore, the argument goes, he must specialize and practise hard, early in life—say, from seven. In fact, there are some notable exceptions—high-class performers who began much later— but the point may be valid in that it would have been much easier for them to learn to use their muscles correctly at a younger age. This means continuous practice when still at school age, not just a lesson a week. The principle is thought to apply to other instruments as well—if one is aiming to reach the very top standard.

It is a very hard decision to commit one's child to a programme of dedication and excellence—given that to do so may deprive him of a chance of high academic success in 'normal' subjects. This must depend on advice from top-level music teachers and performers that the child has what it takes musically as well as technically; on evidence that the child derives a lot of pleasure out of music even when he has been working hard at it; and on a sense of controlled excitement apparent in him when he plays a piece to an audience, large or small. Some would add that he needs to be very intelligent too in a general way—but this is disputable.

All the above can apply equally well to specializations outside the area of performing music as such.

Gay and Lesley are cousins, who both went to a specialist

ballet school. Both had done extremely well at dancing classes between the ages of five and ten; they had taken examinations, they had performed at fêtes and festivals, they had gone on courses for promising young dancers. While other girls of like age had their bookshelves full of horse-lore, these two insisted on being given picture books illustrating the lives of Pavlova, Fonteyn, Ulanova . . .

When they left ballet school, Gay was assured of a place in a corps de ballet with a well-known company. Everybody regarded her as unusually talented, and her dedication was obvious. When Lesley left, she took a secretarial course. Nothing shameful about that: her sense of vocation as a dancer had evaporated. But she is now a business executive, since her company decided she had too many ideas about her work to warrant keeping a typewriter on her desk. She spends her spare time working for an external degree—and curses what she calls the wasted hours at the ballet school. These are not the dancing lessons, because she enjoyed them, and she feels they have been good for her health and her body; but the time spent on music appreciation, costume design, and 'going to a museum just to worship somebody's old shoes'. She admits the fact that she probably helped persuade her parents into their choice of school, but feels resentful that no one drew attention to her moderate talent and moderate motivation, once it became apparent that she was below the best pupils in these respects.

Lesleys as well as Gays are going to be sent to ballet schools, however careful the selection procedure. But the Lesleys could be helped by more watchful observation and assessment of how each child is progressing. This information then has to be acted on, in a practical way.

The argument about young violinists' muscles applies to young dancers as well: they need to be caught young to make their bodies respond suitably to the demands made of them. The question has to be put—how many other specializations deserve or need exclusive preparation early in life? Drama is sometimes suggested. But many fine actors never went to classes in acting, either at school or at college. Many others went to a dramatic art college from an ordinary school or university, after a general education.

This is an area for debate. But on educating children with a view to a dramatic career at least one expert believes that over-training children leads directly to woodenness or stereotyped performance on stage. Barbara Speake believes in providing a *general* education at her school, with the opportunities for learning to move, to speak well, and to organize dramatic events offered on top of this solid basis. This is a different approach, and apparently more realistic than that of the old-fashioned acting school.

In other countries, schools have been established for gifted children with a strong talent for science or mathematics. It is worth contrasting the reported result of this in the USA with what has been claimed for it in the USSR. Almost any case can be made out for or against the principle, depending on the way you interpret the problems that appear to have arisen in the USA, or the total success apparently met with in Russia. In any event, where maths and science are concerned, one asks oneself why it should be necessary to go to the lengths of segregating children to teach them those subjects well. Giving them an enriched diet of maths and science in the context of a normal school seems an entirely satisfactory goal. The same could be said for languages or art.

The gifted child with a highly specialized gift has been considered. Of the high IQ gifted child, with many strings to his bow of a normal academic kind, it can be said that he probably presents the fewest problems, assuming that his progress has been happy as well as impressive to this stage.

He is unlikely to maintain the same degree of motivation all his school career. Sometimes he may pause and query or resent the assumptions made about his winning prizes and scholarships. Intelligent children are bound to wonder whether this is worth while. Both schools and parents are liable to substitute anticipated pride (e.g. 'Our school went up from xth to yth in the Oxbridge entrance league table this year—the sixth form is strong, and we should be able to hold our place') for the principle of helping each child towards a satisfying life. Unhappiness is not satisfying. Hard work by itself has nothing to do with unhappiness. A sense of emotional blackmail coupled with doubt that even the hardest work will suffice, leads directly to it. But provided expectation is kept in proportion to the child's natural competitiveness, there are many schools that will suit this kind of giftedness. But what of the 'creative' diverger? Where on earth should he be sent?

Some private schools allow for, even pride themselves on, a certain amount of free-floating eccentricity among intelligent children. It is revealed in the enthusiasms of head teachers when they talk about their work and their sixth forms. Some examples of this:

Possibly we should have had another award at London University, had not one of our girls felt impelled to discuss the problems of the third world in her paper on economic history. It wasn't the least bit relevant, and they asked me rather stuffily afterwards: 'Is she a firebrand?' They should have understood that she has both intelligence and a character—which is unusual . . . she will shock us all, I'm sure, but we will miss her . . . (Headmistress of a private girls' school in the Midlands.)

Some would have swept this girl under the carpet. But here it was obvious that although she emerged determined to change society, she had been encouraged to probe, to rethink arguments, to develop her ideas.

We can boast an unusual distinction this year—we got one lad into a college of art to study stained glass.

This was a boy who had performed brilliantly when he felt like it, but showed little interest in following through a syllabus. Several teachers had been infuriated by him because he seemed to be entirely perverse in what he bothered to learn. (He knew a lot about Roman cookery, while his Latin Prose would have a sense of style, but little syntax.) In the end, instead of trying to force him into one of the recognized moulds, such as sixth form classics, or history and English, he was allowed to pursue French at an advanced level, and art at several levels—a basic course in art history, and an intensive study of glass and stained glass which he made alone, with occasional guidance from the art master. The latter was one of a minority who did not regard this boy as a figure of fun, and made investigations to see how he could best make progress in his unusual choice of specialization.

It is fairly easy to spot a mood of stern conformity at a school when making a visit to one. It does not matter how good the school's record may be, if it clearly seems off a gifted diverger's wavelength.

Some well-known schools allow an à la carte educational menu for the child who scorns the table d'hôte. These are not much of a muchness, however similar they might seem in not having rules about when or how much to work at a given subject. Philippa's school (see above) became one example of this kind of school where lack of imagination, personality or flair in the teachers results in nobody wanting to do anything except at a superficial level. At other such schools, there is a kind of passionate interest that children demonstrate in what they do. This is related only in a minor way to the facilities available, or to the numbers and nature of the children attending. The deciding factor is a leadership quality that commands interest and inspires children to become involved in projects that will attract attention and approval. A gifted child who seems unable to find something which really engrosses him and stretches his talent to the full often seems to need a special relationship with a teacher. In the right kind of laissez-faire school (i.e. with teachers of character, with many interests, and the power to fascinate children) the creatively gifted child stands a good chance of flourishing.

Too few parents have a thorough look at a school before making a choice. Most are given a conducted tour by the head teacher who is wearing his public relations hat. He shows you the gym, the changing rooms and a language laboratory that seems barely intelligible. Finding out about the atmosphere of a school depends partly on listening to other parents, and to others' children, but must involve a close personal review of the school *at work*. It does not cut much ice to announce to a head teacher's secretary bluntly that your appointment to come on a Sunday afternoon in August is inadequate. This may mean fighting a battle prematurely. A better move is to ask politely if you can come on a weekday during term-time, possibly just as a supplement to your main interview. Where the secretary refuses, the head teacher often gives way—possibly through lack of practice, but probably because he can judge it is not simply idle curiosity on your part. Some parents have found it pays —if other means fail—to turn up on a working day, and apologetically ask to see the head teacher there and then, pleading either a confusion of engagements, or a need to ask 'a few more questions'. Then they ask for another look round.

If you happen to have a gifted child, reflect that *most* schools will *want* him, unless he is emotionally disturbed. Sell him dear, therefore. The subterfuges for getting a satisfactory inspection of a school may not appeal, but you are dealing with an institution that will probably bid for the opportunity to charge you money for taking control over something like five per cent of your child's life.

You may or may not worry about role definition—that is, the sense that children acquire of what is reasonable for them to do and strive for as a girl, or as a boy. But where gifted children are concerned, role definition can be more of a problem. There are few aspects of research among gifted children that are sadder than a comparison of male and female achievements in the follow-up by Terman among gifted children a long time after they had first been identified. It is not surprising, nor is it regrettable, that while many of the men were captains of industry, many of the women were simply housewives and mothers. But those women who were *not* housewives were mostly secretaries. Quite good ones, no doubt. But they seem to have struck an adult patch of 'under-achievement', the counterpart of under-achievement among the gifted at school. Society and business were not prepared in the 1930s for women to use their talents in any way that seemed too masculine.

It is simple to claim that there is more equality of opportunity nowadays. But the sexes are only as equal as they feel. An exceptional child may have pretensions that seem to belong by convention to the other side. The pretensions will seem all the more alarming because he (or she) is *really* talented. But society is suspicious of clever boys with a talent for ballet, and of girls with the mathematics and mechanical imagination to become an engineer. It may be that given your gifted child's *particular* enthusiasm, you will need to choose a school where crossing conventional borders between 'his' and 'her' activities is more often tolerated. Anyone who doubts the extent of this problem only has to consider the relative numbers of men and women students offering arts and science subjects at university; or the fact that of the first twenty names in the list of those who had the best results in the National Mathematics Competition in 1973, precisely one was a girl. A gifted girl, given the barriers and frustrations encountered by intelligent women not only in business, but in government organizations and some areas of the academic world too, is much more likely than the average to become a staunch Women's Lib supporter.

If your gifted child is emotionally disturbed, or has problems in the education area that relate back to bad experiences at his first schools, special counselling is needed. This is available as of right in the Children's Department at your local authority. Of course the level of expertise in dealing with the special problems posed by a minority group of children must vary. They will know of most of the schools which deal not just with giftedness or disturbance, but the two together. There are not many: some are schools which maintain a unit in which such children, alone or in combination with other groups, can receive special teaching. The best known specialist school is probably the Red Hill school, run by Otto Shaw.

There is a big difference between real disturbance and chronic under-achievement. The latter needs a new 'set'— that is, the child has to be encouraged to take a different view of what is expected of him, what he can do, what people he might admire and what they are doing. Changing schools is not a sufficient step, since long-established ways of thinking have to be changed, and work itself needs to be made to seem interesting. This touches on the question of motivation itself, and personality differences between the determined and the casual child. Motivation cannot suddenly be fed through the veins. I hope I have managed to dissuade parents from turning the screw on a child who is simply not interested in academic progress. Tempt him, by all means. But hard pressure, whether physical or emotional, is an attack on his right to be an individual.

Further reading

For a general background to the subject, these two books will be found interesting. The first makes no demands of specialized knowledge. The second is shorter, but provides a more detailed examination of specific aspects, such as problems of IQ and 'creativity' tests.

Gifted Children. Margaret Branch and A. Cash, Souvenir Press, 1966.

The Gifted Child. J. B. Shields, National Foundation for Educational Research, 1968.

A readable but detailed analysis of some of the main paths taken by research on gifted children is this paper:

The Teacher and the Gifted Child. L. Lowenstein, AEP Journal, vol. 3, No. 2, Autumn 1972.

There are two works (one of them a series of studies), which deserve to be called classics. Both are more demanding than anything mentioned so far, but by no means inaccessible to an average reader who is determined to study the field thoroughly:

Genetic Studies of Genius. Vols. 1–5. L. M. Terman *et al*. Stamford University Press (USA), 1925–59.

The Gifted Child. C. L. Burt, British Journal of Statistical Psychology, 14, 2, 123–39, 1961.

Another important book, which was very advanced for its time, is concerned with findings on gifted children in New Zealand. It is still relevant, and worth reading:

Children of High Intelligence. G.W. Parkyn, New Zealand Council for Educational Research, 1948.

A lot of useful information about how different gifted children approach school work, and a very interesting account of organizing 'enrichment' sessions is given in:

Gifted Children and the Brentwood Experiment. S. A. Bridges, Pitman, 1969.

This is helpful to both parents and teachers.

For a vivid description of under-achievement by gifted children, and analysis of what can underlie it, I warmly recommend:

Able Misfits. M. L. Kellmer Pringle, Longman, 1970.

Any reader who wants to make a thorough study of the theories put forward about creativity, and the ways in which gifted creative minds might work, should probably start with Bridges's book (above), followed by:

Contrary Imaginations. Liam Hudson, Pelican Books, 1967.

This is witty as well as being deservedly influential. While it has been criticized, there is a case for including the following as well, on the grounds that it began a movement, and certainly provokes thought:

Creativity and Intelligence. J. W. Getzels and P. W. Jackson, John Wiley and Sons Inc. (USA), 1962.

Finally, here are two papers which give an indication of the situation and problems of gifted children in this country:

Educating Gifted Children. D.E.S. Reports on Education, 48, H.M.S.O., July 1968.

Gifted Children in the Primary School. N. R. Tempest, Paper delivered to British Assoc. for the Advancement of Science, 1970.

Index

not because intelligent.

be what want to be.